VGM Careers for

CAREERS FOR

HIGH-ENERGY PEOPLE

& Other Go-Getters

MARJORIE EBERTS
MARGARET GISLER
MARIA OLSON

SECOND EDITION

VGM Career Books

New York   Chicago   San Francisco   Lisbon   London   Madrid   Mexico City
Milan   New Delhi   San Juan   Seoul   Singapore   Sydney   Toronto

JAN 2 6 2005

297161

The *McGraw·Hill* Companies

Library of Congress Cataloging-in-Publication Data

Eberts, Marjorie
    Careers for high-energy people & other go-getters / by Marjorie Eberts, Margaret
Gisler, and Maria Olson — 2nd ed.
        p.   cm. — (VGM careers for you series)
        ISBN 0-07-143730-4 (alk. paper)
        1. Vocational guidance.   I. Title: Careers for high-energy people and other go-
getters.   II. Title: High-energy people & other go-getters.   III. Gisler, Margaret.
IV. Olson, Maria.   V. Title.   VI. Series.

    HF5382.E23   2004
    331.702—dc22   2004002954

· ·

We would like to dedicate this book to
the bundles of energy in our families—
David, Martha, and Shari.

1 2 3 4 5 6 7 8 9 0   DOC/DOC   3 2 1 0 9 8 7 6 5 4

ISBN 0-07-143730-4

McGraw-Hill books are available at special quantity discounts to use as premiums and
sales promotions, or for use in corporate training programs. For more information, please
write to the Director of Special Sales, Professional Publishing, McGraw-Hill, Two Penn
Plaza, New York, NY 10121-2298. Or contact your local bookstore.

This book is printed on acid-free paper.

Contents

Acknowledgments

· ·

We wish to thank Kevin Crider for substantial help in updating this book.

CHAPTER ONE

Careers for High-Energy People

The sun isn't even up, but you are already going full speed. You have only one speed—high. On the job, you like the fast-paced assignments that keep you on your toes and on the go all the time. You seek out task after task because you like the challenge. Do others fatigue and slow down while you keep going strong? Do you see yourself as a vigorous, vibrant individual with a tremendous capacity for action? Are you bursting with energy from the time you get up in the morning until you crawl into bed at night? If so, you are a high-energy person—a go-getter.

High-energy people are a special breed. They delight in spending as many waking minutes as they can in activities. You'll find them on the job long after less-energetic coworkers have left for the day. Beyond the workplace, you'll discover them playing sports, digging in gardens, remodeling homes, and hiking in the hills. They are the exact opposites of couch potatoes.

As children, these peppy people shied away from television and other strictly sedentary pursuits and released their energy in nonstop activity. You'd see them running exuberantly just because it was fun to run. Many embraced sports with a passion and played on school teams. They were also enthusiastic participants in extracurricular activities, from school musicals to scouting.

Fortunately, for those of you who are high-energy people, there are many jobs that are perfect matches for your strengths. Companies are searching for people who have the energy to work long hours, can stay alert and focused on the job, and love working at a fast pace.

An Amazing Variety of Jobs for High-Energy People

When you start looking for jobs that offer the opportunity to work full tilt all day long, an astounding number of possibilities will emerge. You'll find jobs in just about every career area, from medicine to entertainment, to sports and business. You could work on an assembly line that is moving at a rapid pace or in an emergency room making lightning-fast decisions. You could be a firefighter working for days to put out a forest fire or a messenger riding on a bicycle and delivering one message after another. Navy SEAL, combat soldier, bulldozer operator, Wall Street trader— there is just the right job out there for someone who zips through life with an abundance of energy.

Look at the following want ads. These companies are searching for high-energy people. Note how they use key words such as *energetic, enterprising, vital,* and *enthusiastic* to describe the people they wish to employ.

- **Administrative Assistant.** Motivated and enterprising candidates wanted for rewarding position in diverse and energetic team environment. Professional company seeks polished candidate who thrives in a fast-paced environment. Superb telephone manner and prioritization skills required.
- **Executive Chef.** Ideal candidate has extensive background in fine dining and high volume. We require a vital, energetic, hands-on, and enthusiastic professional with experience in union environment, food, and labor cost control and the ability to handle up to five hundred diners per night at the highest possible standard.
- **Sales Manager.** Publicly traded consumer service organization seeks energetic individual with a keen sense of urgency

to manage Los Angeles sales team of eight individuals. Requires degreed individual with minimum two years' experience managing a sales force.

- **Messenger.** Bike messenger needed for deliveries in financial district. Full-time and part-time positions available. Clean-cut, vigorous, and enterprising are musts.
- **Personnel Recruiter.** This is the time to get into the personnel industry! One of Chicago's oldest and most reputable personnel services companies seeks a high-energy customer service person to join our winning staff of professionals. If you have an entrepreneurial spirit and drive and are motivated, this is the place for you.
- **Hospital Emergency Medicine Group.** This five-hundred-bed hospital is searching for a board-certified eligible emergency medicine physician to join the staff of six full-time physicians. The hospital has an extremely busy Emergency Room with more than sixty thousand visits per year. Day and night shifts are shared equally among the physicians, who work thirteen to fifteen twelve-hour shifts per month. The physician will be paid an hourly rate of $120.

This book is designed to help all those with high energy find a fast-paced job that allows them to use that wonderful reservoir of energy in the workplace. Here is a glimpse of some of the careers that you will read about in this book.

Careers in the Sports World

Sports heroes Derek Jeter, Warren Sapp, and Venus Williams have found energy-burning careers as professional athletes, and so have all the players on soccer, basketball, and ice hockey teams. Fortunately, talented athletes have opportunities to find jobs in more sports and sport franchises each year. While careers as officials, coaches, instructors, and trainers are not usually as glamorous as those of professional athletes, they do require individuals with a great capacity for action. Just think of the energy officials expend as they chase after Shaquille O'Neal or David Beckham, the way coaches enthusiastically direct the action from the sidelines, and the busy days of sports trainers and instructors.

Careers in Law Enforcement and the Military

As long as criminals prey upon the public, and countries and terrorist groups threaten national security, individuals will be needed to protect our lives, rights, and property. The jobs of police officers, sheriffs, soldiers, sailors, marines, and FBI and DEA agents not only demand an abundance of physical energy, but also require the mental energy to face life-and-death situations that can occur without a moment's notice. Some groups, such as SWAT teams, Navy SEALs, and Green Berets, train relentlessly to be prepared to handle the most dangerous missions.

Careers in the Medical World

Medical emergencies require fast attention. Some are handled by busy doctors and nurses in emergency rooms. Others are first dealt with by emergency medical technicians (EMTs) on roadsides, in homes, on mountain slopes, on beaches—wherever emergencies happen. Busy days requiring enormous expenditures of energy aren't just the province of individuals dealing with emergencies. Your own family doctor may work long, draining hours helping one patient after another and then go home to be on call all night. The surgeon may also be on his or her feet as long as twelve hours at a time, performing complicated operations that require total concentration.

Careers in Food Service

When you dine out, you want a good meal and high-quality service whether you are eating in a fast-food joint or white-tablecloth restaurant. Everyone knows that all the employees in fast-food restaurants never slow down on the job. Although it is not as obvious, it is the same story in all restaurants. Waiters spend their shifts on their feet, serving one customer after another. All of the chefs, cooks, and other kitchen workers must work at breathtaking speed as long as there are customers in the restaurant. Food-service jobs are filled by people who must be indefatigable.

Careers in Delivery Services

When it comes to the delivery of letters and packages, the key word is speed. Doubtless, Superman's ability to travel faster than a speeding bullet would make him the ideal delivery service employee. Delivery service jobs require people who can work fast throughout the workday to handle the avalanche of mail and packages that must be delivered every day. Jobs delivering mail and packages are found with the postal service, giant companies such as FedEx and UPS, small delivery companies, and messenger services.

Careers in Entertainment

Entertainers have to work hard to get and keep the attention of the audience. They can't relax for a second when they are in the spotlight because the audience wants to see a spirited performance. It takes energy to be a performer, whether you are a singer like Britney Spears, a comedian like Jerry Seinfeld, a classical musician like Yo-Yo Ma, or a movie star like Jude Law. Behind the scenes, the individuals who are directing, producing, and working on all forms of entertainment must also be energetic because this is a fast-moving world in which new movies, TV shows, concerts, and entertainment must be created quickly.

Careers in the Business World

More people work in business than any other occupation. Within the vast world that produces goods and services, employees who are bursting with energy are especially needed for certain career paths. Salespeople must be driven people—always working for a sale. Stock traders and investment bankers must be dynamic individuals to handle the frenetic pace of stock market transactions and the intense atmosphere of investment banks. And in the technological world, where things are happening so fast that an Internet year is said to be a month in real time, employees work at an unbelievable pace.

Careers in Manufacturing, Construction, and Maintenance

Henry Ford popularized the assembly line in the early 1900s, and since then millions of workers have had jobs putting together one product after another as the parts move down the line at a steady pace. In the construction field, all of the homes, offices, shopping centers, and roads that are built every year require workers who are vigorous and strong enough to handle eight or more hours of intensive labor in these demanding jobs, whether they are driving a bulldozer or swinging a hammer. High-energy people are also needed to maintain homes, offices, shops, and hotels in tip-top condition.

Even More Jobs for High-Energy Types

The number of jobs with high-energy requirements would form a very, very long list. In the last chapter of this book, we suggest ways to find even more of these jobs. Also, we describe a number of ordinary as well as very unusual jobs that are being done by people—from hairdressers to mountain trekkers—who have successfully matched their interests with their boundless energy.

Job Qualifications

High-energy people and other peppy types want to find jobs to fulfill their need to move at full tilt all day long. They consider it essential to be busy and challenged throughout the workday. They are full of life and energy and want to throw themselves wholeheartedly into their careers. Nevertheless, just having energy does not ensure finding a satisfying job. Most jobs today require a considerable skill level. For many jobs, training beyond high school and college degrees is essential to getting your foot in the door. Assembly-line workers, Wall Street traders, and FedEx delivery employees are all operating computers in their work. Paramedics may need as much as one thousand hours of training. Chefs may have attended cooking schools. Even fast-food restaurants have schools for their employees. Fortunately, high-energy types have the energy and enthusiasm necessary for getting the training they need for the jobs they want.

CHAPTER TWO

Punt, Coach, and Announce

Careers in the Sports World

E veryone has dreamed of becoming a professional athlete. We have been inspired and awed by great basketball players like Michael Jordan and Magic Johnson who made the game look easy. High school football players aspiring to play in the NFL look to superstars like four-time Super Bowl quarterback Joe Montana as an example of how to throw the winning touchdown. How about baseball great Mark McGwire? Aspiring players hoping to play in the big leagues strive to develop the skills and the power needed to hit the ball out of the park. And, of course, many of today's soccer fans still remember Pelé, the most brilliant soccer player in history. Young soccer players still practice his famous back dropkick as they try to acquire the skills necessary to join a school or professional team.

Success in the athletic arena can bring fame and glory. The names of many sports stars are well known even by non–sports fans. Everyone has heard of Muhammad Ali, Sammy Sosa, Brian Boitano, Arnold Palmer, Anna Kournikova, Michelle Kwan, and Lance Armstrong. Behind the success of every athlete, whether he or she is a superstar or a lesser-known team player, is a reservoir of energy. You must be indefatigable to run up and down the basketball court, soccer field, or football field; skate continuously in ice hockey games; return countless balls in tennis matches; or race a bicycle. And besides all the time in the public eye, there's the even greater amount of time spent in practice. It takes a tremendous capacity for action to play most sports.

If you truly have talent in a particular sport, you may be lucky enough to convert your dream into a career as a professional athlete, as golf phenomenon Tiger Woods has done. Some athletes, such as Wayne Gretzky, Charles Barkley, and Jackie Joyner-Kersey, have professional careers that have spanned more than a decade, but keep in mind the many others who have had short professional careers because of injury, poor performance, or some other misfortune. Furthermore, relatively few athletes are capable of having careers as professional athletes. High-energy people who are sports aficionados should not think only of a career as an athlete playing in front of a crowd, but also of all the many other careers associated with sports, from being a coach to working as a trainer. There is an even greater number of careers in the sports world for those who may not be able to shoot like Larry Bird or play tennis like the Williams sisters.

Is a Career in Front of the Crowd for You?

If you really believe that you are one of the lucky people who might just have a shot at a career as a professional athlete, taking the following quiz will help you see exactly what is required. Answer the following questions "yes" or "no" to see whether you have most of the characteristics of professional athletes.

1. Do you possess the correct body type for your sport?
2. Do you have the ability to produce results?
3. Do you have a genuine love of the sport?
4. Do you have the ability to listen carefully?
5. Do you have a true talent for the sport?
6. Do you have the desire to continue perfecting your skills?
7. Do you possess a highly competitive nature?

8. Do you have the stamina to survive living on the road?
9. Do you have the ability to get along with all types of people?
10. Do you possess the knack of being tactful and courteous?

Now that you have an idea about whether or not you can handle the job of a professional athlete, here are some more questions designed to let you see if you are capable of handling the mental pressures of this career. Answer these questions "yes" or "no."

1. Are you flexible?
2. Can you make rapid decisions?
3. Do you possess the emotional strength to handle a job full of high excitement?
4. Do you like performing in front of a crowd?
5. Can you adjust quickly to new ways of doing things?
6. Can you handle criticism?
7. Do you react well under pressure?
8. Do you possess the ability to handle defeat?
9. Can you handle frustration?
10. Do you possess emotional control?

Thinking About Your Qualifications

Answering yes to every one of the twenty questions above does not necessarily mean that you will be happy or successful as a professional athlete. There are many additional qualifications for each sport. Playing a sport is the best way to determine whether a sport is for you. Reading about the lives of professional athletes can also be helpful in learning more about what it takes to succeed in this career.

The Story of a Professional Soccer Player

Matt Coyer started playing soccer at the age of six and played professional soccer for the Indiana Twisters. If you have ever seen a soccer game, you know how physically demanding it is, as the players literally never stop running. According to Matt, you need energy not just on the field, but also for handling practice sessions and all the public-appearance work.

It was evident in high school that Matt was destined to have a future in soccer, after he led his team to a state championship and was a two-time all-state player. From high school, he went on to play college soccer at Indiana University, playing on back-to-back Big Ten championship teams. Out of the seventeen players who were recruited his freshman year, he was the only one to play four straight years.

Matt was attracted to a career in professional soccer because he loved the game and wanted a career doing something that he was passionate about. Before joining the professional ranks, he played on the Indiana Men's Select State Team that won a national championship and trained with the United States National B Team. He finds his career to be challenging as he is continually learning more about playing soccer and trying to play better. Matt knows that as a professional in any sport, you are only as good as your last season and must constantly strive to become a better player. The thing that Matt likes least about his career is that it is not a year-round job. He only plays for five or six months, and then he needs to find other employment. In the off-season from November through April, Matt does community relations for the Twisters.

A Typical Day on the Job. Matt arrives at the soccer training center by 8:00 A.M. He has to be on the field ready to practice from 9:00 A.M. until noon. If he has an injury, he needs to spend time with the trainer to get the necessary treatment. After practice the players have some free time, then they have appearances at different youth soccer camps. Matt usually gets home around 7:00 or 7:30 P.M., unless he has a game. Also, depending on the team's playing schedule, he may be traveling as much as three or four days a week.

Career Advice from Matt. For those who want to follow in his footsteps in becoming a professional soccer player, Matt advises:

1. Practice skills by yourself to become a better player.
2. Be prepared to learn when you go to team practice.
3. Try to play against better players. You can learn a lot from watching someone who is more skilled than you are.
4. Study the game by watching the game being played.

In addition, Matt believes that you need to have dedication, natural athletic ability, and assertiveness to be a good professional athlete.

After his professional career is over, Matt believes he will still be involved with soccer in some way, whether it is coaching, playing in a recreational league, or just watching a lot of soccer on television.

What It's Like to Be a Pro Football Player

Mike Prior began playing professional football in 1985 with the Tampa Bay Buccaneers. Mike, an amazingly talented athlete, lettered in football, baseball, and wrestling in high school and received a football scholarship to Illinois State. In college he played both football and baseball and attained such recognition for his skills that he was the fourth-round draft pick of the Los Angeles Dodgers and a seventh-round draft pick of the Tampa Bay Buccaneers.

Mike played with Tampa Bay for two seasons; however, he was sidelined most of the second season with an injury. He then played for six seasons with the Indianapolis Colts, where he enjoyed such accomplishments as three interceptions in a game and ninety-one tackles in a season. He especially remembers running back an intercepted pass thrown by Bernie Kosar for a touchdown. Mike then played for the Green Bay Packers for five seasons. If you watched the 1997 Super Bowl game, you saw Mike intercept a long pass in the second quarter when the game was still very close. Mike's career is very unusual because the average professional career is only three or four years.

What Mike likes best about his job as a professional football player is having to organize only six months of his life around the team, and then having six months off. However, he does spend time in the off-season conditioning for the next season. The Green Bay Packers have three minicamps in April, May, and June to ensure that the players are getting in shape for the football season. What Mike likes least about his job is attending all the meetings and having to deal with the media.

Mike's Views on a Football Career. Mike was first attracted to a career as a professional football player because he had a talent for the sport and loved to compete. He believes that to be successful, professional football players must have physical ability and talent, be able to think on the field, and truly understand the game. According to Mike, one of the most challenging things for a professional football player is keeping your composure.

After his professional career, Mike hopes to coach football and even baseball at a high school. His advice for anyone wanting to follow in his footsteps is to get an education. He points out that it is great to realize your dreams and become a player; however, careers can end abruptly and nothing can ever take away an education if football does not work out.

Sports Careers for Those Who Are Not Professional Athletes

The multimillion-dollar sports industry provides a wide variety of career opportunities besides being a professional athlete. The industry needs energetic people in positions such as business manager, referee, publicist, trainer, scout, coach, physical therapist, marketing coordinator, sales and ticket manager, mascot coordinator, director of statistical information, sports broadcaster, and sportswriter, as well as careers in community relations, media relations, and human resources. Some of these jobs are filled by retired professional athletes whose love of sports compels them to stay around the action. Most, however, are filled by people with various backgrounds who want to be a part of the sports world. The rest of this chapter will give you a bird's-eye view of some of these careers that demand a vigorous effort.

The Enforcers of the Rules

Every sport needs an equalizer. This job falls into the hands of the official. Whether it's throwing a flag for roughing the passer, signaling a foul and counting the bucket, or calling a base runner out, an official's job is to add continuity to the game. Officiating at any level is a true test of the character, energy, knowledge, skills, and fitness of the officials who make split-second decisions while enforcing the rules. This is definitely a career for a sports lover who falls into the high-energy category. Referees in some sports run almost as much as the players and must never let their attention waver from the action for a minute.

Take the following quiz to determine whether you have what it takes to be an official. Answer "yes" or "no" to these questions:

1. Are you able to handle verbal abuse with tact?
2. Can you keep your composure when everyone around you is upset and the scene is chaotic?
3. Can you make accurate split-second decisions?
4. Do you have good eyesight?
5. Do you have good health and a high level of fitness?

Should you decide to become an official, it is important for you to understand that you will usually have to start at the bottom of the ladder and work your way to the top. This means, for example, officiating for years in class A, B, or C baseball before making it to major league games. It also means a lifestyle of working evenings and holidays while living much of a season out of a suitcase.

If you are serious about pursuing a career as an official, you may wish to subscribe to *Referee* magazine (P.O. Box 161, Franksville, WI 53126). For more information, you can visit the website at www.referee.com. In each issue of the magazine, you will learn about what is happening in officiating, read profiles of successful officials, and find out ways to improve officiating skills. The magazine also provides information about annual clinics for officials. There are no special education requirements for becoming an official; however, some officials have found it helped their careers to attend an officiating school. Contact the following associations for more information about officiating schools:

BASEBALL
Jim Evans Academy of Professional Umpiring
12741 Research Boulevard, Suite 401
Austin, TX 78759
www.umpireacademy.com

BASKETBALL
The Referee School
P.O. Box 51924
Boston, MA 02205
www.therefereeschool.com

FOOTBALL
National Federation of State High School Associations
P.O. Box 690
Indianapolis, IN 46206
www.nfhs.org

Coaches: Directing the Action

Coaches are needed for team sports such as football, baseball, soccer, and basketball. In these sports, there are also jobs for assistant coaches and positional coaches. Coaching positions can be found at a wide variety of competition levels, from junior high school to the professional ranks. Coaches are involved in training players, developing game strategies, recruiting new players, and directing play during games. This leads to very long, action-packed days during a season. While you may not see the energy coaches expend in practice, you can clearly see how much energy they burn during games as they pace the sidelines, constantly confer with coaches and players, and signal plays. Also, travel is involved at all levels of competition.

Coaching opportunities are not limited to team sports. In some individual sports, such as tennis and golf, players may have full-time or part-time coaches. Athletes in sports such as figure skating and gymnastics also have coaches who are essential to their training. Some coaches have achieved as much fame as well-known players. Sports fans know the names of former Indiana University basketball coach Bobby Knight, former San Francisco Forty Niners football coach Bill Walsh, and former Dodgers baseball coach Tommy Lasorda.

No special degrees are needed to be a coach except at the junior and senior high school levels, where it is necessary for full-time school employees to be licensed teachers. Use the following questions to determine whether you have the same characteristics as successful coaches:

1. Do you possess good people skills?
2. Do you have a solid knowledge of the sport?
3. Do you possess leadership abilities?
4. Do you have excellent communication skills?
5. Do you have the ability to work under pressure?

Earnings and Advancement

Coaches at junior and senior high schools are paid according to the teachers' pay scale, which averages around $40,000 a year. Many of these coaches also receive a stipend from the school for being coaches, and some may receive additional money from booster clubs. At the college level, coaches of major sports in successful sports programs can earn salaries in the hundreds of thousands of dollars. The income of coaches of professional teams is closely allied to the popularity of the sport, the success of the team, and the reputation of the coach. Good coaches can earn several million dollars a year.

Typically, coaches begin as assistant coaches at high schools or colleges. Sometimes they begin as position coaches with professional teams before advancing to positions as head coaches. Head coaches climb the career ladder even further by moving to larger schools or more prestigious professional teams. Successful college coaches often move into the professional ranks.

More Information About Coaching

You can obtain more information about coaching careers by contacting the following associations:

National Youth Sports Coaches Association
2050 Vista Parkway
West Palm Beach, FL 33411
www.nays.org/IntMain.cfm?Page=1&Cat=3

National High School Athletic Coaches Association
P.O. Box 4342
Hamden, CT 06514
www.hscoaches.org

A Personal Perspective on Coaching

Dan Kapsalis has been a soccer coach for sixteen years. He played soccer all through high school and walked onto the Indiana University soccer team. You will find that most coaches have played the sport that they coach. After college, Dan played in an amateur soccer league, started a soccer store, and coached soccer at several levels, including high school, Olympic development, soccer camps, and club programs.

As a high school soccer coach, Dan finds being around young people and being a positive influence in their lives is one of his biggest rewards as a coach. There really is nothing he doesn't like about coaching; however, he does find it very time-consuming. In order to be a good coach, Dan believes that you need to have good communication skills for working with young people plus personal experience in playing the sport. He points out that you have to be able to motivate players and teach them both the technical and tactical side of the game. According to Dan, you also need leadership and organizational skills, patience, and the ability to handle criticism from those who try to second-guess you. Besides coaching on the field, he finds there is a lot of administrative paperwork, medical forms, and game and transportation schedules that need to be completed.

Dan enjoys seeing the young people he coaches go on to the next level, as well as knowing that he has helped them along the way as players. The most challenging part of being a coach for Dan is not winning or losing but seeing how much he can help every player on his teams improve.

Athletic Directors

The tremendous popularity of sports has brought so many sports and levels of competition to schools that it has become necessary for colleges, senior and junior high schools, and even some elementary schools to hire athletic directors to oversee their sports programs. Typically, athletic directors have been coaches and have good supervisory, administrative, communication, and interpersonal skills. At the junior high and senior high levels, they also have teaching or administration certification and act as the primary conduit for communication among the administration, coaches, athletes, parents, and community, as well as handle the scheduling of events. At the college level, athletic directors play a major role in hiring coaches, scheduling events, publicizing sports events and personnel, and financing the school's sports program.

At all levels, they work closely with coaches and are concerned with how they can help coaches do their jobs better. They also have to be facilitators, able to resolve conflicts. Because they play so many roles in their jobs, athletic directors need to have great stores of energy.

An Athletic Director at a High School

Lee Lonzo started at a suburban high school in Indiana as a social studies teacher and head boys' tennis coach. Today, he is the school's athletic director. His daily schedule clearly shows that this is a job with high-energy requirements. Lee works from 7:30 A.M. to 9:30 P.M. Monday through Friday and all day on Saturday. Then Lee usually has more paperwork to do on Sunday, along with booster club meetings. Being an athletic director really means having the equivalent of two jobs. It is largely an office job from 7:30 A.M. to 4:00 P.M. on weekdays. Then it turns into a job supervising sports events evenings and Saturdays.

On a typical day, Lee is constantly juggling phone calls, administrative work, paperwork (contracts for a thousand athletic events a year), and visits from coaches, teachers, athletes, school administrators, parents, vendors, and boosters. He also handles discipline as it relates to the sports teams. Included in his workday is a forty-five-minute stint doing cafeteria duty. And after school, he attends sports contests almost every day.

....

Trainers

Did you know that athletic trainers were once the people who coached college athletes? Today's trainers, however, are not concerned with coaching but with injury prevention and rehabilitation. When a player is injured, the athletic trainer goes into action, designing a treatment program and then making sure that the athlete follows the program. No longer is all the trainer's work done behind the scenes in the locker room. You will find trainers at sporting events taping and icing injuries to help players return to the game.

Becoming a trainer usually requires the completion of specific courses, and in most states a trainer must be licensed in order to practice this profession. Most trainers work for professional sports teams, college teams, and high school teams; however, some trainers work for hospitals and clinics that hire out their services to teams and schools. You can learn more about this career by contacting the National Athletic Trainers Association at www.nata.org or the American Physical Therapy Association at www.apta.org. There is considerable competition for positions as trainers, especially at the college and professional levels.

On the Job as a Trainer

Gwen Van Ryen took the first step toward her dream of becoming an athletic trainer by working as a student trainer during her four years in college. Today, she is working a forty-hour week as a physical therapist/athletic trainer in the physical therapy and sports medicine clinic of a hospital. To get this job she needed to have a bachelor's degree in physical therapy plus certification through the National Athletic Trainers Association. This certification requires specific course work plus between eight hundred to fifteen hundred hours of experience as an intern before the certification test can be taken. Gwen also had to be licensed by the state as a physical therapist. Besides working at the clinic, she is also working from five to thirty hours a week as a trainer at a large suburban high school.

At the clinic, Gwen deals primarily with patients who have orthopedic and sports injuries. After her clinic job is over on weekdays and Saturdays, this busy trainer works at the school in the training room, on the playing fields, and at sports events covering home games and selected away events. This part of her job involves the prevention, evaluation, treatment, and rehabilitation of athletic injuries. Gwen is able to provide emergency care for injuries and follows through until athletes are fully returned to the sport. Due to the large number of athletes at the school, she tends to be quite busy getting athletes ready for practice and evaluating and rehabilitating injuries.

Daily Routine in the Fall. Here's a close look at one of Gwen's action-packed days in the fall. It begins early in the morning.

7:00 A.M. Begin work in the clinic—directing patient care.

3:30 P.M. Leave clinic to work as trainer at school for soccer and other team games.

4:00 P.M. Begin taping athletes competing in the games; evaluate previously injured players; assemble ice, water, and emergency supplies on the playing field; introduce self to opposing coaches and advise them of emergency procedures.

4:30 P.M. Games begin (usually two, but could be three), plus three other teams practicing—cover all events; assist with any injuries sustained in play or practice.

6:30 P.M. Games end—continue to cover practices, perform rehabilitation with athletes as needed, write up daily reports, make injury evaluations, discuss injuries with parents and coaches, and make a log of all athletes seen and services rendered.

7:30 P.M. Gather supplies and return them to car or appropriate school facility.

8:00 P.M. Arrive home.

8:30 P.M. Restock supplies kit, as needed; finish paperwork.

Instructing Adults and Children in Sports Skills

For so many sports, you are right in the heart of the action when you teach sports skills. You may be hitting balls to a fledgling tennis player or a seasoned pro, showing a golfer or swimmer the correct way to do a stroke, or spotting a gymnast trying to learn how to do back flips. Most sports instructors have actively played in the sport they teach. Often, they have reached a high level of expertise in that sport. But sports instructors must also develop teaching skills. This can be done by attending classes and workshops given by sports associations and colleges. Sports teachers can then keep their skills updated by reading magazines, books, and newsletters in their sports areas, watching instructional videos, and attending teaching sessions at workshops and conferences. Besides knowing teaching techniques and having a genuine desire to teach sports, instructors need to help players develop confidence in their abilities.

A Tennis Club Instructor

P. A. Nilhagen was an excellent junior tennis player. Today, he is the director of Junior Development for one of the largest tennis programs in the United States as well as a tennis instructor for both private and group lessons. At times, his days may start as early as 5:00 A.M. and continue until as late as 11:00 P.M. You have to be very vigorous to sustain such a demanding schedule, especially when you are spending quite a bit of your time hitting balls to players and demonstrating proper techniques.

This tennis pro's background includes a bachelor's degree in physical education as well as certification by the United States Professional Tennis Association (USPTA). P.A. continues his tennis education by regularly attending USPTA conferences and conventions. He also subscribes to eight tennis magazines, reads every available tennis book to learn more about the sport, and studies videotapes of televised matches.

P.A.'s advice to prospective teachers or coaches of any sport is to make sure that you love your sport and the people who you will be training in that sport. He also suggests finding a role model who you can emulate. Finally, P.A. believes that sports teachers should stay fit and dress professionally.

Owner of a Gymnastic Facility

Terry Spencer reached the top in women's gymnastics as a member of the 1968 U.S. Olympic gymnastic team. Unfortunately, she had to leave the squad because of a sprained ankle. After Terry's competitive gymnastics career was over, she briefly promoted gymnastics for the owner of several gymnastics camps before opening her own gym. When she first started her gym, she worked from ten in the morning until one in the afternoon and then returned to the gym at four and stayed until ten at night. On weekends, she would take students to meets or host meets at her gym. Terry points out that being the owner of a gym requires one special aptitude—stamina. She stresses that you must have the strength to handle the staff, parents, and children, as well as all the problems related to running a business. Terry's gym has succeeded wildly; she now has a staff of thirteen and more than five hundred students attending classes. With success, she has trimmed back her teaching hours to between 4:00 P.M. and 10:00 P.M. and spends her mornings doing paperwork.

....

Sports Announcers

There is no possible way even the most avid sports enthusiast can attend every game. So to keep up with all the scores and play-by-play action, many sports lovers rely on radio and television sports announcers to keep their knowledge of what is happening in the sports world up-to-date. Becoming a sports announcer is highly competitive. Quite often, you start in another position at a radio or television station and advance by proving you have an aptitude for "on-air" work. Because sports announcers work on tight deadlines, you must be ready to ad-lib all or part of a show. And if you are doing play-by-play coverage of a game, you must describe what is happening as soon as it happens. This is a high-pressure job requiring a peppy person who can interject enthusiasm into his or her broadcasts. In radio, sportscasters' average annual salary is about $53,300. In television, salaries may start at about $32,000 and top out at over $100,000 per year. You can learn even more about careers in sports broadcasting by contacting:

National Sportscasters and Sportswriters Association
P.O. Drawer 559
Salisburg, NC 28144
www.nssahalloffame.com

Dan Kapsalis, the soccer coach whom you read about earlier in this chapter, has started to broadcast his city's professional soccer games on radio. Dan finds it challenging to always be speaking when the light is on. He feels it is essential to practice diligently just as athletes do before a game.

CHAPTER THREE

Patrol, Investigate, and Protect

Careers in Law Enforcement and the Military

A rmed robbery in progress! With lights flashing and sirens piercing the air, police cars descend on the scene. Guns are drawn, and the suspect is taken into custody. Meanwhile, a thousand troops race across the desert battlefield in their armored vehicles to stop the advance of a ruthless dictator. The police and the military have the challenging job of enforcing the laws, keeping the peace, and protecting the people of the nation.

Today, local, state, and federal law enforcement personnel protect our lives and property within the country while the military has the responsibility of deterring aggression from other countries or militant groups. Capturing criminals, apprehending fugitives, preventing crimes, participating in military operations, rescuing distressed vehicles at sea, and preventing smuggling—all are activities that require a considerable capacity for action. High-energy types can find many careers within law enforcement and the military that will place almost superhuman demands on their energy levels. These are careers that demand not only physical energy, but also mental energy in facing life-and-death situations, from rescuing hostages to engaging in military combat. There are the well-publicized jobs of daring SWAT team members and Navy SEALs, as well as the less-glamorized jobs of foot soldiers and officers on the beat.

A Career in Law Enforcement

Law enforcement officers spend their time in different ways. Many officers spend the majority of their time interviewing witnesses and suspects, apprehending fugitives and criminals, collecting evidence, and providing testimony in court. Correctional officers are responsible for the care of those who are incarcerated. Other officers spend most of their time patrolling a beat to preserve the peace and to prevent crime.

Along with the excitement and tension that can flare up at any moment in these jobs is the paperwork all law enforcement officers are required to file. Here is a closer look at some of the varied jobs law enforcement officers hold:

- **Local police and law enforcement officers** have general law enforcement duties ranging from directing traffic at the scene of a fire to investigating a burglary.
- **Officers in large police departments** usually are assigned to a specific detail for a fixed length of time, such as motorcycle patrol, canine corps, or emergency response team.
- **Sheriffs and deputy sheriffs** have duties resembling local police departments and generally enforce the law in small departments in rural areas.
- **State police officers** patrol highways and enforce motor vehicle laws and regulations. They are often called state troopers or highway patrol officers.
- **Drug Enforcement Administration (DEA) agents** work for the federal government and specialize in enforcement of drug laws and regulations.
- **Federal Bureau of Investigation (FBI) agents** are the principal investigators of the government. They may investigate violations of federal laws in connection with bank robberies, kidnapping, espionage, or terrorism.
- **U.S. Border Patrol special agents** protect more than eight thousand miles of international land and water boundaries.

Their primary mission is to detect and prevent smuggling and the unlawful entry of undocumented aliens into the United States.

- **U.S. Secret Service special agents** protect the president, vice president, and their families and investigate counterfeiting, the forgery of government checks or bonds, and the fraudulent use of credit cards.

What It Takes to Work in Law Enforcement

First of all, if you want to work in law enforcement, you are most likely to work in a large police department because that is where most of the jobs are. To become a candidate for a job, you usually must pass a competitive written examination. You also need to meet rigorous physical and personal qualifications and be at least twenty years old. You usually must have a high school diploma; however, more and more departments want candidates to have some college training or military experience. And almost every job with the federal government requires a college degree.

Obtaining a job in law enforcement is not a matter of luck but rather the result of hard work, endurance, and completing all the required steps in the process. Many of today's law enforcement workers come from a military background because military experience is directly transferable to law enforcement careers. Military life is more regimented than civilian life, and members have learned to accept discipline and the more stringent dress and grooming requirements. Furthermore, during times of conflict, military personnel may find themselves in life-or-death situations. In addition, countless hours of training produce teamwork that is highly critical to the success or failure of an operation, and possibly to the lives of individuals in the unit. These skills learned in the military are definitely necessary when working in most law enforcement careers, especially in the area of corrections.

Earnings

The law enforcement personnel who earn the highest salaries are those who work with agencies of the federal government and often earn 25 percent of their money from overtime work. Federal agents hired at the GS-10 grade earned an annual base salary of about $41,000, but with overtime they earned just over $50,000 per year. On the local level, the average salary of nonsupervisory police officers and detectives is about $42,000 a year, while supervisory personnel average about $61,200 a year.

The Story of a Deputy

Douglas E. Milligan was first attracted to a career in law enforcement back in the fifth grade, when his oldest brother became a military policeman. That is exactly what he wanted to do, and so he followed in his brother's footsteps after a year of college and became a military policeman. After three years, he left the army and worked in security for a large department store. He continued his climb up the ladder by getting a job as a security supervisor at a hospital. His current job is as a special deputy for a school, and he has the ambition to become an investigator. To enhance his career opportunities, he has attended a law enforcement academy. Douglas has the career background of many law enforcement officers.

The Backbone of Law Enforcement

Belonging to a special weapons and tactics (SWAT) team, a bomb squad, or a search-and-rescue team are definitely exciting law enforcement jobs. However, these are not the high-energy jobs that the people in the community see on a daily basis. People in the community see and are in direct contact with the officers who patrol their streets, respond quickly to their calls for help, and are always on the lookout for criminal activities. These law enforcement officers are the true backbone of crime prevention.

The Story of a Patrolman

Police work is done around the clock. Patrolman William Haymaker works from 10:45 P.M. to 7:15 A.M. His basic duties are to patrol neighborhoods and business districts. At the same time, he is responsible for maintaining traffic control and responding to call assignments. These assignments could be a burglary in progress, a domestic quarrel, a suicidal subject, or a call from the owner of a lost dog. He never knows what a call will bring and must always stay alert as he responds to them. William is also part of the local SWAT team and could be forced to respond at any time to calls that are not handled by regular patrol officers. These are higher-risk assignments. He is also a field training officer for new employees and a defensive tactics instructor. This combination of responsibilities makes it essential for William to have a reservoir of energy to draw upon in the diverse situations he encounters.

Behind Bars: Careers in Correctional Facilities

Today, there are more than 6.7 million inmates in correctional facilities, and, unfortunately, it appears that this number will continue to increase, fostering a need for even more correctional officers. These are the law enforcement officers who have daily contact with offenders, maintaining security and observing inmate conduct and behavior to prevent disturbances and escapes. This job calls for someone who is alert at all times, as correctional officers must be prepared to quickly handle and defuse any situation that arises.

The job of correctional officers is to make sure inmates are orderly and obey rules. In order to do this, they monitor all the activities of the inmates, including working, exercising, eating, and bathing. Sometimes, they have to search inmates and their living quarters for weapons or drugs. They also settle disputes between inmates and enforce discipline. They must never show favoritism and must report any violation of the rules.

Working Conditions and Earnings

Correctional officers work in a high-stress environment under constant pressure. Nothing is ever normal in a prison, whether the officers are supervising inmates, patrolling the grounds, or standing guard high up in a watchtower. Anyone thinking about a career in corrections must realize that at any given time, a calm, day-to-day routine can shift to a very intense situation at the drop of a hat. That is a reality of this job.

Because prison security must be provided around-the-clock, correctional officers work rotating shifts of eight-hour days, five days a week. You'll find them working in state and federal penitentiaries, institutions for the criminally insane, reformatories, detention centers, and prison camps.

Where you work as a correctional officer influences how much you will earn. Correctional officers in state facilities earn an average annual salary of $33,200. Federal correctional officers earn about $38,900 per year, while officers at local facilities earn about $31,400 per year. The average yearly salary for supervisors is about $45,200. Most officers are provided with uniforms or given a clothing allowance, and all have a solid benefits package.

Looking at the Job of a Correctional Officer

David Wayne Hardwick preenlisted in the Marine Corps a year before he graduated from high school. For part of the three years that he was in the service, he was team leader for a security platoon, gaining experience that would be helpful later on in his career. After David left the service, he worked at a variety of jobs until his brother, who was working in corrections, got him interested in a career in this area.

For twelve years David has been a correctional officer at a state prison facility. Because he is a go-getter, he has also taken on the additional responsibility of becoming a trainer. He holds special training certificates in firearms, personal protection, restraint equipment, transportation of offenders, and forklift operation. David trains almost every new officer who comes to work at the facility. In addition, this very energetic person is a member of the emergency squad (E-Squad). All members of E-Squad received specialized training, passed a special physical examination that is repeated every six months, and must attend an additional eight hours of training every month. As a member of E-Squad, David can be called any time there is a major disturbance, hostage situation, or escape. The facility has three different E-Squads of approximately fifteen men each. All the squad members carry beepers so they can respond quickly in the case of a crisis. David does not receive extra benefits or pay for belonging to this special squad, but he feels satisfaction in knowing that E-Squad members are always there if fellow officers need help.

A Typical Day for David. When David enters the facility to begin a shift, he empties all his pockets, walks through a metal detector, and is patted down (searched) for weapons and other prohibited items. Next, he goes to the roll call desk to get any necessary information for the day and then walks back to the control room to get his keys and radio before going to his assigned job area—the food industry. He checks each offender who comes to work in the area, watches them change clothes for their job, and then searches them. During his shift, he calls departments (medical, dental, other) to check out the authenticity of offenders' passes. At 10:30 A.M., all the offenders who are going to eat early have to be patted down. Then at 11:00 A.M. daily, a security check of the entire institution is made, which means David must count all the offenders in his area. After the count clears and a signal is given, he watches the offenders who have finished their work for the day strip and change clothes. Again, he must pat them down before they leave. After his lunch, he continues to watch offenders until it is time to count the offenders again. Then his shift is over, and he turns in his keys and radio.

David's Insights About His Career. David does not hesitate to say that he was scared to death the first day on the job. Today, he feels that he is very well suited for all the jobs he does because of the excellent training he has received and continues to receive. To be a good correctional officer, David says, it is essential to be able to talk to and understand individuals with backgrounds that are very different from your own.

It is also necessary, he believes, to have common sense. Furthermore, he points out that officers must be alert at all times to keep the facility secure. According to David, you always must know what is going on around you.

Learning More About Law Enforcement

These organizations can provide helpful information about careers in law enforcement.

National Association of Police Organizations
750 First Street NE, Suite 920
Washington, DC 20002
www.napo.org

National Sheriffs' Association
1450 Duke Street
Alexandria, VA 22314
www.sheriffs.org

American Correctional Association
4380 Forbes Boulevard
Lanham, MD 20706
www.aca.org

The Military: America's Largest Employer

If you become a member of our armed forces, you will be working for the largest employer in America. Because of its size and mission, the military offers educational opportunities and work experience in literally thousands of occupations. There are more than two thousand basic and advanced military occupational specialties for enlisted personnel and sixteen hundred for officers. And the best part about it is that 75 percent of these occupational specialties have civilian counterparts. Of course, not all of these jobs are ones that demand an energetic performance from the jobholder. Nevertheless, there are many, including combat soldier and Special Forces personnel, that require vigorous people with a great capacity for action.

When you join the nearly 1.5 million people who are serving in the armed forces, you are part of a group whose mission is to

1. Deter aggression and defeat attack against the nation
2. Strengthen and build alliances
3. Prevent a hostile power from dominating a region critical to our interest
4. Prevent conflicts by reducing sources of regional turmoil through various means, including providing humanitarian aid, countering terrorism, or limiting the spread of significant military technology

Each department of the military has different responsibilities. The army and air force prepare for defensive and offensive operations, on land and in the air, respectively. The navy organizes and trains forces primarily for sea operations, while the Marine Corps, part of the Department of the Navy, prepares for land invasions in support of naval or amphibious operations. The Coast Guard, under the Department of Transportation (except in wartime, when it serves with the navy), enforces federal maritime laws, rescues distressed vessels and aircraft at sea, operates aids to navigation, and prevents smuggling.

Factors to Consider in Deciding on a Military Career

Before deciding on any career, including the military, it is important to know as much as you can about exactly what is involved to avoid surprises. First of all, the military places these demands on its personnel:

1. When you sign an enlistment contract, you have signed a legal document that obligates you to serve for a specified period of time.
2. You will be required to follow stringent grooming requirements.
3. The needs of the military always come first, so your working hours and conditions can vary enormously.
4. Rigid formalities will govern many aspects of your everyday life. You will salute senior commissioned officers and address them as "sir" or "ma'am."
5. You must obey the commands of your superiors immediately and without question.
6. You may be required to travel, live in cramped quarters, have lengthy overseas assignments, and even be in combat situations.

However, you need also to weigh these very positive aspects of military service in making your decision:

1. You will enjoy more job security than your civilian counterparts.
2. Satisfactory job performance generally assures one of steady employment and earnings.

3. Living expenses and full health care coverage will be available for you and your family.
4. You will have the opportunity for adventure and travel.
5. You will be eligible for retirement benefits after twenty years of service.
6. After you leave the service, you will be entitled to veterans' benefits that will help you buy a home or receive money for your continuing education.

Basic Military Pay

The salaries of military personnel are based on their rank and years of service. Most enlisted personnel start as recruits at Grade E-1, which has a monthly salary of $1,104, while commissioned officers started at Grade O-1 and a monthly salary of $2,264. Individuals with special skills or above-average education may start at higher grade levels.

The Life of an Air Force Navigator

With the lure of flying on the horizon, Dennis Wimer elected to follow a career in the air force after graduation from college. He has flown all over the world as the lead navigator on a Lockheed C-141B Starlifter. His flight days are always action packed, and Dennis has been exposed to combat and hazardous situations during his time in the air force, as his unit has aided in the peacekeeping mission in the former Yugoslavia. If Dennis and his crew did not work well together in these situations, it might have resulted in the loss of their lives. These are the times when it is essential for military personnel to have the ability to sustain a high level of energy.

A Dangerous Mission in Bosnia. During the war in Bosnia, Dennis flew one of the first C-141Bs into Sarajevo to deliver critical food and medical supplies. Since all power was out at the Sarajevo airport, the specialized electronic equipment that guides airplanes to a safe landing was not operational. Therefore, the crew had to develop its own approach into the airfield, avoiding mountains and possible small-arms fire from the ground. Before the flight, the officers studied the planned route into Bosnia and then onto the airfield. The intelligence officers informed the crew that the Serbians had placed a large weapon on the hillside just outside of Sarajevo, and it was capable of shooting down the plane if it were just a fraction off course. As navigator, it was Dennis's primary task to ensure proper course alignment. He could see the large weapon aimed at the plane throughout the entire approach into Sarajevo. Fortunately, the crew landed the plane with no damage and proceeded to unload the cargo to the United Nations peacekeepers. In a peaceful situation, it takes two to three hours after landing to be ready for departure. In this case, the crew landed, taxied to parking, downloaded thirty-two tons of cargo, taxied back to the runway, and took off in just fifteen minutes. The rest of the crew depended on Dennis's navigational skills to guide them safely into Sarajevo, and he depended on their skill to land the aircraft and download the cargo as quickly as possible. Only with complete crew coordination, effective communication, and an energetic effort could this mission have been accomplished.

Another Hazardous Situation. In the effort to be always ready to go do their job, Dennis and fellow crew members train in some very dangerous situations. An exercise in Nevada brought together fliers from all over the free world to practice wartime scenarios. During one specific training flight, the crew was trying to avoid being shot down by an aggressor aircraft, an F-15 acting as a Russian MiG. During the maneuvering to avoid getting shot, the plane's altitude went from three hundred feet above ground level (AGL) to eighty feet AGL. The wingspan on the C-141B is eighty feet. As Dennis began to look inside the airplane, he noticed the altitude just as the pilot flying the airplane announced that he was going to make a hard turn to the right and told the crew to hang on. Dennis immediately yelled at him to initiate a climb. It took three loud yells and a quick hit on the back of the head for the pilot to stop his turn and begin to climb. While practicing procedures that would save the crew in a real wartime fight, they almost flew the airplane into the ground, which would probably have killed the entire eight-man crew. This exemplifies the importance of all crew members staying alert at all times.

The Elite Combat Forces of the Military

When the military has difficult and dangerous missions to perform, it calls upon special operations teams. These elite combat forces stay in a constant state of readiness to strike anywhere in the world on a moment's notice. Special operations forces team members conduct offensive raids, demolitions, intelligence, search-and-rescue, and other missions from aboard aircraft, helicopters, ships, or submarines. Due to the wide variety of missions, special operations forces team members are trained swimmers, parachutists, and survival experts. Together, all the services have approximately forty-six thousand special operations team members who have some of the most action-packed jobs that exist in either military or civilian life. These jobs are perfect for high-energy people in search of adventure.

Each year approximately thirty-nine hundred new members are picked to train for special operations forces. If you were selected for this elite combat force, you would have to complete up to seventy-two weeks of formal classroom training and practice exercises. The content of your courses would typically include:

- physical conditioning, parachuting, swimming, and scuba diving
- using land warfare weapons and communications devices
- handling and using explosives
- disposing of bombs and mines

Additional training would occur on the job, and your basic skills would be kept sharp through frequent practice exercises under simulated mission conditions.

A Look at Very Demanding Duties

Special operations forces team members in the military are called upon to perform some or all of the following duties:

- Go behind enemy lines to recruit, train, and equip friendly forces for guerrilla raids.
- Carry out demolition raids against enemy military targets, such as bridges, railroads, and fuel depots.
- Clear mine fields, both underwater and on land.
- Conduct missions to gather intelligence information on enemy military forces.
- Conduct offensive raids or invasions of enemy territories.
- Destroy enemy ships in coastal areas using underwater explosives.

Strenuous Physical Requirements

The difficult nature of the special operations forces requires very demanding physical requirements. Good eyesight, night vision, and physical conditioning are required to handle mission objectives in parachute, overland, or underwater activities. Excellent hand-eye coordination is also required for the detonation or deactivation of explosives. In most instances, special operations forces team members are required to be qualified divers, parachutists, and endurance runners.

Are You a Good Candidate for the Special Operations Forces?

You have probably seen the activities of special operations forces in many movies and television shows. Some films, such as *Navy SEALs*, do give a fairly realistic picture of what you might be expected to do in this very demanding career. Ask yourself the following questions to see whether you have the right attributes to consider joining a special operations force.

1. Can you work as a team member in all types of circumstances?
2. Are you ready to accept the challenges of this job and face danger?
3. Can you stay in top physical condition?
4. Are you able to stay calm in highly stressful situations?
5. Will you be able to acquire the requisite skills?

You really need to answer "yes" to all the above questions in order to consider seriously a job with the special operations forces.

A Glimpse at the Work Environment

Because special operations forces team members must be prepared to go anywhere in the world, they train and work in all climates, weather conditions, and settings. They may dive from submarines or small underwater craft, parachute from planes, or crawl through jungles. Special forces team members may also be exposed to harsh temperatures, often without protection, during missions in enemy-controlled areas. Most of the time, however, they work and train on military bases or ships and submarines.

A Life of Adventure as a Navy SEAL

After graduating from law school when he was twenty-six years old, William (Billy) Mathews wanted far more than to be another lawyer sitting behind a desk. He wanted to have adventure stories to tell his children. Accompanied by a friend, he went to a recruiting office to sign up to become a Navy SEAL. This organization is one of the most feared and respected commando forces in the world. Most of its missions are unknown and unreported. Typically, SEALs operate in small units of one or two individuals up to a platoon strength of sixteen.

The recruiter suggested that Billy apply to officer candidate school. The competition for becoming a Navy SEAL is exceedingly keen, so Billy felt very fortunate to receive one of the three officer candidate school positions as a SEAL. At the same time, he was nervous about successfully completing the rigorous SEAL training program. Besides the SEAL training, Billy also trained at the Army Training Center in Fort Benning, Georgia, for jump school and went to California to learn how to drive a SEAL Delivery Vehicle (SDV), a tiny submarine. Because of his Navy SEAL training, Billy can scuba dive, sky dive, shoot weapons, work with explosives, and drive a minisub on the bottom of the ocean.

There are a total of eight SEAL teams and two SDV teams. Billy was assigned to the team stationed in Norfolk, Virginia. He has been everywhere, from underwater in the Caribbean to the top of the Pyrenees Mountains in Spain. Billy was deployed to the Mediterranean twice, has seen most of Europe, and has worked with special commando units in all the Mediterranean countries.

Through his experiences with the SEALs, Billy has learned to appreciate the job security that a military career offers. He has also discovered that doing his job well can lead to advancement. While travel is one of the major pleasures of being a SEAL, it is also one of its greatest hardships, as it takes him away from home. Billy's advice to anyone who truly wants to be a Navy SEAL or join any of the other special forces is, "Don't quit. Things are not always as bad as they first seem."

Learning More About the Military

Recruiters have up-to-date information about military careers and can explain the many career options to those who are interested. Each of the military services publishes handbooks, fact sheets, and pamphlets that describe entrance requirements, training and advancement opportunities, and other aspects of military careers. These publications are widely available at all recruiting stations, most state employment service offices, high schools, colleges, and public libraries. You will also find helpful information in the following publications.

Military Careers: A Guide to Military Occupations and Selected Military Career Paths, published by the U.S. Department of Defense, 1400 Defense Pentagon, Room 3A750, Washington, DC 20301.

Air Force Times, Army Times, and *Navy Times*, independent weekly newspapers, published by Army Times Publishing, 6883 Commercial Drive, Springfield, VA 22159. Copies are available in recruiting offices and in libraries on military bases or by subscription.

You can also find more information on military careers at the following armed forces websites:

United States Marines: www.marines.com
United States Air Force: www.airforce.com
United States Army: www.goarmy.com
United States Coast Guard: www.gocoastguard.com
Today's Military: www.todaysmilitary.com

CHAPTER FOUR

Rescue, Treat, and Comfort

Careers in the Medical World

Jobs in the medical field require individuals who possess an abundance of energy, have incredible stamina, and can think quickly. Everyday doctors, nurses, and emergency medical technicians are on the front lines of medical treatment, dealing with emergencies such as heart attacks, severe injuries, or allergic reactions. These medical professionals have to work quickly to treat life-threatening situations. Often they must move from one emergency situation to the next with little or no break. They work in hospital emergency rooms, surgical recovery rooms, and intensive-care units. They are also the people who work for ambulance services, fire departments, police forces, and rescue squads. You probably have an idea about the pace and pressures of these jobs from watching popular emergency room and rescue shows on television. These, however, are not the only jobs in the medical field requiring individuals with a great abundance of energy. There are many other doctors and nurses who regularly work long hours helping one patient after another in busy medical offices, clinics, and hospitals.

Doctors Past and Present

In the distant past, it was witch doctors and medicine men who were called to help people recover from illnesses because they had magic or knew the appropriate rituals. One of the first to separate medicine from magic and superstition was Hippocrates, a Greek physician and the father of modern medicine. He taught that illness had its own cause, and physicians had the responsibility to find the cause. The Hippocratic oath that many graduating medical students take today is named for him.

Unlike their recent predecessors, today's newly trained physicians face radically different choices of where and how to practice. Many new physicians are less likely to enter solo practice and more likely to take salaried jobs in group medical practices, clinics, and HMOs in order to have regular work hours and the opportunity for peer consultation. Others take salaried positions simply because they cannot afford the high cost of establishing a private practice while paying off student loans.

Physicians must have an abundant supply of energy, as most work long, irregular hours. Sixty-hour or longer work weeks are common for doctors. Only as physicians approach retirement age do they accept fewer new patients and tend to work shorter hours.

On the job, physicians diagnose illnesses and prescribe and administer treatment for people suffering from injury or disease. Physicians also examine patients; obtain medical histories; and order, perform, and interpret diagnostic tests. They also counsel patients on diet, hygiene, and preventive health care.

It's Not Easy to Become a Doctor

The journey to becoming a doctor is long and arduous. It typically takes as long as eleven years: four years of college, four years of medical school, and three years in residency. And it can take even longer for some specialties, which may require up to eight years of residency. Because entrance to medical school is so competitive, successful applicants have to earn excellent grades in challenging college courses and receive a solid score on the Medical College Admission Test (MCAT). Then after the first two years of intensive study of such subjects as anatomy, biochemistry, microbiology, and pharmacology in medical school, students begin to work with patients under the supervision of experienced physicians. The residency experience, lasting from one to seven years, places extreme demands on young doctors with extraordinarily long hours (on call for twenty-four-hour stretches) and a very heavy workload. Finally, before becoming a physician, it is necessary to pass a difficult licensing test. This career path challenges even the most energetic individuals.

Job Outlook and Earnings

The employment of physicians is expected to grow about as fast as the average for all occupations through the year 2010 due to continued expansion of the health care industry. New technologies permit more intensive care. Physicians can do more tests, perform more procedures, and treat conditions previously regarded as untreatable. In addition, the population is growing and aging, and health care needs increase sharply with age. However, because of current efforts to contain medical costs, a smaller percentage of specialists will be in demand.

Physicians have among the highest earnings of any occupation. According to an American Medical Association report in 2002, the average annual income after expenses for all physicians was about $160,000. Surgeons earned the highest average yearly income of $240,000, and pediatricians earned the lowest average yearly income of $126,000. The average yearly salaries of residents ranged from $36,500 for those in their first year of residency to $46,300 for those in their eighth year.

An Emergency Room Doctor's Challenges

The doctor in an emergency room setting faces one of the most challenging and fast-paced jobs around. K. Douglas Marshall, M.D., is chairman of the emergency department at a metropolitan hospital, where he spends his days dealing with a variety of life-threatening conditions running the gamut of medicine, from pediatrics and obstetrics to geriatrics and trauma problems. Dr. Marshall never has a "typical" day. Some days are very light and some are incredibly heavy, with several patients arriving at the same time.

Doug finds one of the great challenges of his job is trying to meet people's expectations. Many people think emergency rooms are designed to handle patients with ongoing problems, when the only thing that can be done is to direct them to other medical resources. He is also faced with people who expect the same fast service at emergency departments that they receive from the drive-up window at fast-food restaurants—not accepting that emergency room services must be prioritized according to medical need.

In his job, Doug saves lives as he helps people through critical situations. He finds it immensely satisfying to resuscitate a patient and know that the individual will be able to walk out of the hospital and have a productive life. When Doug is in the emergency room, he is the only physician. However, he does not feel that he works alone because he has a team of nurses working with him.

Career Advice. Doug points out that his job is a difficult one. There is considerable burnout in this career because the stress level is high, and the doctors definitely do not have normal working hours. In choosing a medical specialty, he advises future physicians to study hard and to let their choices evolve through their experiences.

More Facts About Emergency Medicine Careers. According to the American Medical Association, fewer than 3 percent of all physicians are specialists in emergency medicine. If you look at postings of job openings, it becomes clear at once that these doctors work long shifts and all hours of the day or night because many hospitals have twenty-four-hour emergency departments. Emergency medicine doctors may be expected to work twelve-, twenty-four-, or even seventy-two-hour shifts. And in extremely busy emergency rooms, the doctors oversee the visits of thousands of patients in a year.

A Brief Look at Trauma Teams

Trauma teams are designed to provide a safe and efficient evaluation of patients with multiple injuries. They identify all injuries and begin the management of the injuries. Time is of the essence in the work of trauma teams. Ideally, a trauma team at a hospital would have no other duties than to receive and treat trauma patients, but this is not possible at most hospitals because it is simply too expensive. A trauma team may consist of the following personnel: team leader, anesthetist, general surgeon, orthopedic surgeon, emergency room physician, nurses, radiologist, and individuals who provide ancillary services, such as running samples to labs. With a trauma team, it is essential that everyone know his or her place and tasks. The team leader directs the team members in their actions.

More Busy Physicians

It is not just emergency room physicians who have their days crammed with excitement and activity. Many doctors need to be high-energy people to handle their large caseloads and long hours. Furthermore, physicians' days do not end when they see their last patients. Many are on call in the evening and on weekends, when they must talk to patients with medical problems and even go to hospitals to visit them. And certain specialties, such as orthopedics, require doctors to be ready at any time to handle emergencies, from broken arms to fractured hips.

A Tireless Pediatrician

Dr. Gustave "Stavie" Kreh works along with seven other doctors in what is one of the largest pediatric practices in the Southeast, with more than twenty-five thousand patients. Their office opens at 9:00 A.M., 365 days a year, and stays open until every child has been seen, which could be as late as 8:00 P.M. On weekends and holidays, only two doctors are in the office. The group also has two satellite offices.

Stavie starts his day at 6:00 A.M., when he checks with his answering service for messages from patients and reports from partners. Then he is off to visit the two hospitals that the group services, where it usually takes him anywhere from one to two hours to visit his patients and confer with the nurses on each patient's progress or any potential medical problems. Around 9:00 A.M., Stavie arrives at the office, where he sees an average of forty patients a day. On an extremely busy day, he may see up to eighty patients. While seeing so many patients may seem like assembly-line doctoring, Stavie says that most children have illnesses that are easily treated, including headaches, colds, and infections of the ears, respiratory system, and skin. When the occasional emergency arises, Stavie immediately goes to the hospital to take care of the child. He also spends time attending conferences, monthly pediatric meetings, staff meetings, and hospital committee meetings, as well as business meetings related to the practice.

The Grind of Medical School. Stavie attended the Louisiana State School of Medicine in New Orleans after graduating from college. Medical school, he says, teaches the facts and the how-to that every pediatrician needs, but he believes that his liberal arts degree is what gave him the foundation to be an excellent doctor. He wants students who are contemplating becoming doctors to realize that medical school is a tough grind even for students who did well in high school and college. Most medical students are overwhelmed by the tremendous amount of study and memorization that is required their freshman year.

Stavie still remembers the first day of medical school, when he could not even pronounce the words on the professor's mimeographed handouts. Challenged by the difficulty and amount of work that was required of him, he battled back by studying eight to ten hours a day in class and then four or five more hours in the library at night, proving that high-energy people can achieve their dreams.

"By the end of the intense, four-year medical program," Stavie points out, "you are like a sculpture. You have been chiseled, beaten, sat on, molded, melted down, and refined into a finished product." But the sculpture was not yet finished—he then had to complete a three-year residency in pediatrics. When he recalls those years, Stavie remembers "horrendous hours, lousy pay, and twenty-four-hour duty every third day."

Surgeons Are Busy People

A look at the days of Dr. Tom Southern, a plastic surgeon, clearly shows how difficult it is for this busy person to get everything done that he wants to do. Every Monday and Wednesday, Tom is in his office, seeing patients from nine to five. However, these days do not begin at nine. Before office hours, he visits patients in two hospitals, and after office hours, from 5:00 to 7:00 P.M., he resumes patient visits. On Tuesday, Thursday, and Friday, Tom is in surgery working from 8:00 A.M. until as late as 6:00 P.M. Added to his regular schedule are the three times a month he is on call in the hospital emergency room. Plus, he has to take his turn on call in his own private practice.

As a plastic surgeon, Tom works with trauma and burn cases and does reconstructive and cosmetic surgery. What Tom likes most about plastic surgery is the variety of surgical procedures that he performs and the different personalities of his patients. His advice to anyone who is planning to enter the medical profession, and especially plastic surgery, is to be prepared to immerse yourself in your job—but find time in your busy schedule for yourself and your family.

Emergency Medical Technicians

Automobile accident injuries, heart attacks, near drownings, unscheduled childbirth, poisonings, and gunshot wounds all demand urgent medical attention. It is the job of emergency medical technicians (EMTs) to give immediate care and then transport the sick or injured to medical facilities. Being an EMT is a job for an individual who has very special skills, an ability to stay calm in emergencies, and the energy to handle a high-pressure job dealing with life-or-death situations. EMTs, who usually work in teams of two, follow instructions from a dispatcher and swiftly drive specially equipped vehicles to the emergency scenes. If necessary, they request additional help from police or fire department personnel. EMTs determine the nature and extent of the injuries or illness while also trying to determine whether the patient has epilepsy, diabetes, or other preexisting medical conditions. EMTs then give the appropriate emergency care, following strict guidelines as to which procedures they may perform.

All EMTs can handle certain procedures, such as opening airways, restoring breathing, controlling bleeding, administering oxygen, treating for shock, assisting in childbirth, treating and assisting heart attack patients, and giving initial care to poison and burn victims. EMT-Intermediates, who have had more advanced training, can also handle other intensive-care procedures, including administering intravenous fluids and using defibrillators to give lifesaving shocks to stopped hearts. EMT-Paramedics, who have had still more training, can give even more extensive prehospital care; they can administer drugs orally and intravenously and interpret electrocardiograms.

While one EMT drives a patient to a medical facility, the other monitors vital signs and gives additional care as needed. Some EMTs work for hospital trauma centers or jurisdictions that use helicopters to transport critically ill or injured patients. At the emergency department, EMTs tell the staff their observations and the care they have provided. They may even help provide emergency treatment. Then after each run, the EMTs clean the vehicle, replace used supplies, and check the equipment.

A Look at Employment and Earnings

EMTs work for private ambulance services, municipal fire departments, police forces, rescue squads, and hospitals. Employment opportunities for EMTs are growing faster than for most occupations. The most competition for jobs will be in fire, police, and rescue because of attractive pay and benefits and good job security. What EMTs earn depends on their level of training, experience, and workplace. The average annual salaries are EMT-Basics, $31,320; EMT-Intermediates, $31,550; and EMT-Paramedics, $37,700. Paramedics who work at fire departments earn the highest salaries.

EMT Training Is Challenging

You must have formal training to become an EMT. For EMT-Basic, it is 100 to 120 hours of classroom instruction plus ten hours of internship in a hospital emergency room. The next step, EMT-Intermediate, requires thirty-five to fifty-five hours of additional instruction, while EMT-Paramedic training courses generally last between 750 and 2,000 hours. If you want to work in a fire or police department, you will also need to be qualified as a firefighter or police officer. By passing examinations at each level and having a certain amount of work experience, EMTs can get state or national certification, which can be helpful in obtaining higher-paying jobs.

A Paramedic's Career Story

Don Herron, an EMT-Paramedic, took the basic EMT class at a local hospital when he was still in high school. After graduation, he completed a six-month paramedic certification class at the University of Iowa. Don then worked as a volunteer EMT for a few months before being hired as a full-time EMT-Basic. During the next year, he worked his way up the career ladder to the highest level, EMT-Paramedic. EMTs work shifts, and their hours fluctuate greatly depending on need, time of year, and day of the week. Don works a regular forty-hour week.

According to Don, when you go to work in this job, you never know at what pace you will be working. Also, there is a lot of waiting that comes with the job; however, once a call has been received, the job becomes very fast paced and stressful. During the fast-paced times, he must be able to react quickly and keep a level head.

Don answers calls with a partner; however, once he is at the scene, he can also be dealing with the fire department, the police, other EMTs, local people, and family members, as well as the patient. According to Don, the greatest challenge for an EMT is dealing with the frantic people at the scene. You are expected to do so many things at the same time: you have to find out who the victim is, talk to family members and calm them down, listen to what happened to the person, communicate with the police, and determine how the accident took place. And as you are doing all these things, you are assessing the victim's problem and providing emergency aid.

Career Advice. Don likes the variety in his job and receives a sense of accomplishment from helping others. In the future, he would like to earn certification as an instructor so that he will be able to share his knowledge with others. Don feels that those who want to pursue this career should take as many health, science, and chemistry classes as possible in high school. He also suggests they participate in "explorer" programs offered by local EMT agencies and hospitals to gain actual firsthand experience in seeing what an EMT does. If they're still interested, they should take the basic EMT course as soon as they are eligible to do so in order to get an early start on their career.

Registered Nurses

Just like the doctors with whom they work, nurses, whether they are registered nurses (RNs), licensed practical nurses (LPNs), or nursing aides, have jobs that keep them on their feet and on the go throughout their shifts. Nurses especially need energy to cope with the rigors of working in emergency rooms, operating rooms, and intensive-care units.

Two out of three registered nurses work in hospitals, where they are usually assigned to one area, although some rotate between departments. Nurses are concerned with the "whole person"—the physical, mental, and emotional needs of their patients. They observe, assess, and record symptoms, reactions, and progress; assist physicians during treatments and examinations; administer medications; and assist in convalescence and rehabilitation. RNs also develop and manage nursing care plans; instruct patients and their families in proper care; and help individuals and groups take steps to improve or maintain health. While state laws govern the tasks RNs may perform, it is usually the work setting that determines day-to-day duties.

RNs must graduate from an accredited nursing school and pass a national licensing examination to obtain a nursing license, which is required for employment. Most nurses have associate's degrees from community college programs or bachelor of science degrees from four-year colleges.

What the Future Holds for RNs

Job prospects in nursing are good. Employment of registered nurses is expected to grow faster than the average for all occupations through the year 2010, and because the occupation is large, many new jobs will result. This growth is being driven by technological advances in patient care, which permit a greater number of medical problems to be treated, and an increasing emphasis on primary care. The intensity of nursing care is increasing, with more nurses required per patient. While there will always be a need for traditional hospital nurses, a large number of new nurses will be employed in home health, long-term, and ambulatory care settings. The opportunities will be best for those with advanced training.

Earnings for RNs

Nurses' earnings depend upon where they work, with those in hospitals and medical centers earning the highest salaries. The median annual salary of staff nurses in these settings, based on a forty-hour week and excluding shift or area differentials, is about $44,800. The average minimum annual salary is $31,890, and the average maximum annual salary is nearly $54,000. Staff nurses in chain nursing homes have median annual earnings of about $41,330. Many employers offer flexible work schedules, child care, educational benefits, bonuses, and other incentives.

A Nurse In Cardiac Surgery

Joyce L. Buenning, RN, is the operating room specialty coordinator for heart and lung transplant surgery at a large metropolitan hospital. Her career demands that she have the energy to be ready to work at any time. Joyce's day often starts in the middle of the night when an organ becomes available for a transplant. Although there is no such thing as a typical day in this job, Joyce usually arrives at the hospital about 6:30 A.M. and stays until 4:00 or 5:00 P.M. She has to make sure that all the equipment and special medical supplies are available so everything is ready for transplants. When an organ becomes available, Joyce must coordinate the removal of the organ from the donor with the readiness of the recipient. Speed is of the essence in transplant situations. Joyce must carry a phone with her at all times in case she needs to come to the hospital for a transplant. When she is all caught up on her paperwork and no transplants are scheduled, this busy, highly skilled nurse is in the operating room helping with emergency heart surgery.

Joyce points out that it is essential to have high standards in everything she does. "In my job, I must be willing to put out," she says. "I must make an extra effort even in the middle of the night because a transplant is the patient's only chance to live."

For More Information

Some of the best sources for more information on the careers discussed in this chapter are medical associations. These groups offer general information on education, training, financial aid, and specific careers.

PHYSICIANS
American Medical Association
515 North State Street
Chicago, IL 60610
www.ama-assn.org

EMTS
National Association of Emergency Medical Technicians
P.O. Box 1400
Clinton, MS 39060
www.naemt.org

National Registry of Emergency Medical Technicians
P.O. Box 29233
Columbus, OH 43229
www.nremt.org

NURSES
National League for Nursing
61 Broadway
New York, NY 10006
www.nln.org

American Association of Colleges of Nursing
One Dupont Circle NW, Suite 530
Washington, DC 20036
www.aacn.nche.edu

CHAPTER FIVE

Cook, Serve, and Cater

Careers in Food Service

"Thank you for choosing McDonald's. May I take your order?" That is what more and more families are hearing. Their busy lifestyles make it much more convenient to eat out. In fact, one in three meals are now eaten away from home. As a result, the restaurant business is one of the fastest-growing businesses in the United States. The restaurant industry is the largest private-sector employer with more than twelve million employees nationwide. The National Restaurant Association predicts that 2004 sales in the restaurant industry will exceed $440 billion, a 4 percent increase over the previous year. There are two main types of restaurants competing for customers: sit-down restaurants, which seat customers at tables and give them menus, and fast-food restaurants. Since 1994, sales in fast-food restaurants have surpassed those in sit-down establishments.

People go to fast-food restaurants for their speedy service, and there simply isn't an employee in a McDonald's, Burger King, Wendy's, or Taco Bell who isn't on the go throughout his or her shift. Being energetic is really a qualification for employment at a fast-food restaurant, whether you are starting as an entry-level worker or as an assistant manager. What many people don't realize is that waiters and waitresses, cooks and chefs, and kitchen workers in almost every restaurant need to be every bit as energetic as fast-food workers to handle these demanding jobs.

Jobs serving and preparing food are not limited to restaurants. Just think about all the schools, hospitals, prisons, company cafeterias, and other places that serve food every day. Also, caterers prepare and serve food for parties and other special events given by individuals and companies.

A Look at Jobs in Sit-Down Restaurants

When you work at a sit-down restaurant, you are either a front-of-the-house or a back-of-the house employee. Typically, those working in the front of the house have contact with customers, while back-of-the-house employees cook and prepare food and clean the equipment. The quality of service these employees provide determines in part whether a patron is likely to return or not.

Can You Meet the Challenge to Be a Waiter?

Customers expect fast and efficient yet courteous service from their waiters. In fine restaurants with formal service, meals are served at a more leisurely pace; however, waitpersons are busy providing many services to each table. For example, they may prepare and toss a salad or flame a desert at the table. In less formal restaurants, the pace for waiters never lets up as they seat patrons, take orders, pour beverages, and serve meals. They may even set up and clear tables and act as the cashier. Decidedly, you must have a vivacious personality and considerable energy to handle this job effectively. It's not easy to be on your feet all the time: carrying heavy trays of food, dishes, and glassware; remembering orders; and engaging in friendly banter with customers.

If you work as a waiter, your job is more likely to be part-time than full-time, and you will be expected to work evenings, weekends, and holidays. Since most sit-down restaurants are small, opportunities for promotion are rather limited. Some waiters advance to supervisory positions, such as maitre d', dining room supervisor, or restaurant manager. Nevertheless, restaurant jobs should never be thought of as dead-end jobs, as two-thirds of those who own or operate a restaurant today worked their way up from lower-level positions. According to the National Restaurant Association, 34 percent actually started out as a busser, dishwasher, or server.

Earnings and Job Opportunities. There are close to two million waiters in the United States today. Most get their income from a combination of hourly wages and customer tips. How much an individual makes depends greatly on where he or she works. You will make the most money as a waiter in popular restaurants and fine dining establishments, largely because these employees receive more in tips. The average weekly earnings, including tips, of waiters is about $320, with the top 10 percent earning about $537.

There will be abundant job openings for waiters through 2010, as the population gets older and many shift from eating in fast-food restaurants to sit-down establishments. Because so many waiters leave the occupation every year, job openings are usually plentiful in good economic times.

A Waitress in a Popular Restaurant. Piatti Ristorante is a delightful Italian restaurant with a menu of interesting dishes. Christine Martinez works five days a week at the restaurant, from 11:00 A.M. to 3:00 P.M. or noon to 4:00 P.M. She is a very experienced waiter with more than fifteen years of experience. On the job, she wears black pants and a white shirt with a tie, which she provides, and a large white apron provided by the restaurant. At the start of her shift, she checks her ten tables to make sure they are set properly and that the chairs are clean. Christine also goes over the day's specials with the chef. At lunch, people wish to be served quickly, as they have a limited amount of time. This means that Christine must make every step count. For example, when she picks up a salad for one table, she'll take a beverage or dessert to another table. During the heavy lunch period, there's scarcely time for her to take a breath as she rushes to serve an entree at one table and a salad at another, greet new customers, and then ring up a credit card.

In busy restaurants, waiters truly work at full tilt during their shifts. Besides serving, Christine acts as a de facto public relations person for the restaurant, giving customers such a good experience that they will want to return. She is also a salesperson, suggesting certain dishes or beverages to her customers. At the end of her busy shift, Christine makes sure that her station is properly stocked for the next shift. Then she checks out the sales she has made on the computer and gives the totals to the manager before leaving.

What It's Like to Be a Chef or Cook

When people go out to eat in sit-down restaurants, the quality of the service is important, as is the quality of the food. Customers want perfectly cooked fish and meat, fluffy mashed potatoes, and delicious pastries. People return time and time again to restaurants that have a reputation for serving good food. And it is the back-of-the-house employees, the chefs, cooks, and other kitchen workers, who are responsible for the quality of the food.

While many people use the terms *chef* and *cook* interchangeably, the chef has more extensive training and responsibilities, including setting the menus for the restaurant. Cooks generally have more limited skills and work under the direction of the chef.

Special Attributes. To be a successful chef or cook, you must have an interest in food, as well as a keen sense of taste and smell. You should be interested in concocting new recipes and staying current with food trends. You also need to know how to lead the kitchen workers whom you will be directing.

Duties. Chefs and cooks have the ultimate responsibility for the preparation of meals. In restaurants, they usually prepare a wide selection of dishes for each meal, cooking most individual servings to order. Their responsibilities also include directing the work of other kitchen workers, estimating food requirements, and ordering food supplies. They may also plan meals and develop menus.

Training. You can start working in a restaurant kitchen with no experience as a kitchen worker and, through on-the-job training, learn how to be an assistant or short-order cook. But if you want to be a chef or cook in a fine restaurant, many years of training or schooling are required. More and more chefs and cooks are now obtaining the training they need through high school or post-secondary school vocational programs and two- or four-year college programs. Training in these schools is mostly hands-on, and you'll learn to bake, broil, and otherwise prepare food, and to use and care for kitchen equipment. You may also take courses in menu planning, purchasing food supplies in quantity, and selecting and storing food. Those who don't want to attend classes can receive training through apprenticeship programs offered by culinary institutes, industry associations, and trade unions.

Advancement and Earnings. As chefs gain a reputation for their cooking, many move from one job to another to acquire better-paying positions. Some chefs can advance to executive chef positions or supervisory or management positions. This is particularly true in hotels, clubs, or larger, more elegant restaurants. Some eventually go on to own their own restaurants. The more elegant the restaurant, the higher the pay a chef or cook receives. Executive chefs may earn more than $45,000 a year, while superstar chefs can earn more than $100,000. On the other hand, the median hourly earnings of cooks are between $7.50 and $10.00.

On the Job with a Chef. After majoring in hotel and restaurant management in college and serving as an apprentice cook for three years, Dieter Puska, an Austrian, came to the United States to work as a chef. In 1976, he opened his own restaurant, the Glass

Chimney, which has been widely acclaimed for its excellence. The energy required to own and operate a restaurant in its early days is almost beyond belief. On a typical day, Dieter would arrive at his restaurant by 7:00 A.M., check the supplies ordered on the previous day, and begin to start lunch. Because his restaurant featured fine dining and gourmet dishes, some sauces would need to cook from two to eighteen hours. After cooking lunch with the assistance of one helper, he would pitch in to clean the kitchen and do the dishes before starting preparations for dinner, which would be served between 6:00 and 10:00 P.M. Then it was another hour or two of cleanup before he could leave.

After a year and a half, Dieter employed more helpers, which relieved him of some of the responsibilities, but he created the menu and was the chef. In 1980, Dieter opened a more casual restaurant, Deeter's, next door. Then he joined with a friend to start an even more casual restaurant, Deeter's & Gabe's. His days are still filled to the brim with activity. Now he stops at Deeter's & Gabe's by 8:30 A.M. to write the specials and check that everything is running smoothly. Then he goes to his office at the Glass Chimney to handle the paperwork involved in running three restaurants. During the afternoon, Dieter checks on the operation of the Glass Chimney and Deeter's. He is the executive chef of these restaurants and is no longer cooking all the time. During the evening, he supervises the operation of both of these restaurants. On his way home, he stops by Deeter's & Gabe's once again before arriving home about midnight. For people wishing to follow in his footsteps, he advises them to take classes, work in good establishments, and try to get a lot of hands-on experience.

Jobs in Fast-Food Restaurants

It seems incredible, but fast-food restaurants that are simply everywhere today have only been around since 1921, when the first White Castle restaurant was started in Wichita, Kansas.

McDonald's birth was in 1948, and Wendy's opened in 1969. Just as it was in the beginning, the goal of fast-food restaurants today is to serve food to customers quickly, efficiently, and economically. The *fast* in *fast food* describes the work pace at all fast-food restaurants. There is no time to sit and rest between tasks, whether you are an entry-level worker or the manager of a restaurant. And if the pace ever slackens, it's time to clean. You truly need to be indefatigable to handle this job. All want ads for fast-food workers should read: Wanted—high-energy people.

A Unique Opportunity to Advance

The fast-food industry is a unique one because energetic people can realistically rise from entry-level positions to restaurant manager and beyond. You can start as an entry-level worker and be promoted to shift leader, then to assistant manager, and finally to manager within a restaurant. From there it's possible to become area, then district manager, and perhaps even president of a fast-food chain. This is the route Edward Rensi, a former president and CEO of McDonald's, took. Furthermore, nearly 60 percent of all McDonald's restaurant managers started as crew members. There is also the possibility of purchasing a franchise and owning your own fast-food restaurant. Instead of starting as an entry-level worker, you can start higher up the ladder if you have attended a two- or four-year college.

Earnings

Once hourly workers in fast-food restaurants were hired at minimum wage, and that was it. But labor shortages in many areas, plus the need for more skilled workers, have made starting wages more competitive with other entry-level jobs. The base salary of restaurant managers is about $31,400 a year. Bonuses increase the salaries of many managers. Some fast-food managers make considerably more than this. There are even managers of very successful units making more than $50,000 a year.

The Pace of an Hourly Fast-Food Worker

As a fast-food worker, you may take orders from customers standing at counters or driving up to a window, and then fill the orders and accept payments. Or you could be preparing and packaging food items, from hamburgers to fried chicken. Whatever you do, you will be working fast to ensure a customer is served swiftly. You must have stamina to be a fast-food worker.

Linda Adams was an hourly worker at a small Dairy Queen that normally employed only three workers on a shift, plus a manager. She never sat down. At times, she operated the cash register, took orders, and filled the drink orders for customers. During peak periods, Linda also assembled orders. At the end of her shift, she cleaned the dining room as well as stocked such things as spoons, napkins, cups, and dessert dishes for the next shift. Sometimes Linda was a back-of-the-store worker, cooking food on the grill. Then she also cleaned the back area, which meant cleaning the floors and the large walk-in refrigerator. In addition, she cleaned the bathrooms, took out garbage, and put new linings in garbage pails. Linda was also sometimes assigned to wash windows, sweep outside, and clean video games.

Assistant Managers

Climbing the career ladder at a fast-food restaurant to the managerial level does not slow the pace of jobs at fast-food restaurants. After working as an hourly employee and then a shift leader in college, George Monroe became an assistant manager at a restaurant that employed thirty workers. His hours were long. He worked seven to twelve hours a day, five days a week, on different shifts.

When George worked the opening shift, his day began at 6:00 A.M. The first thing he did was to make a to-do list of all the things that needed to be done that day. Then he was ready to start his day, which meant counting money from the day before, making out a deposit slip, putting the money in the bank, and picking up the day's change. The next step was to check the time cards from the night before. Then George inspected the entire restaurant, following a company checklist. He also ordered food supplies and checked the dates of existing supplies. He had to do all of this by 10:00 A.M. so he could start to prepare for the lunch rush, which started at 10:30. This meant assigning workers to stations and making sure everything was ready, from lettuce to cheese.

During lunch, George always pitched in to serve the customers wherever he was needed. Then after lunch, he adjusted the number of workers and counted the money and all the items in the waste box (the patties, pieces of cheese, and other items that couldn't be sold because they were dropped on the floor or held too long). George finished his busy day by continuing to work on his to-do list. At the end of his shift, he brought the assistant manager of the next shift up-to-date on what had been happening earlier in the restaurant.

A Glimpse at Jobs in Institutional Food Service

You'll find just about the same jobs at institutional food service facilities as you will in restaurants. All need chefs and cooks, servers, and kitchen workers. The work setting is quite different, however, because it could be a college campus dining room, a hospital kitchen, a prison facility, an armed forces mess hall, a nursing home, or a company dining room. The work is just as fast paced as it is in a restaurant, but you may not have to work evenings or weekends at some facilities. One of the big advantages of working full-time for large food service facilities is the possibility of receiving an excellent benefits package.

A Look at a Career in Catering

You are a cook, server, party planner, flower arranger, owner of a business, and much more when you are a caterer. You handle every single detail in planning, preparing, and serving food for weddings, company meetings, and other festive events. You also need to be a go-getter because you need to find new clients until you have built such a solid base of customers that word-of-mouth recommendations bring you all the business that you can handle.

Before an event starts, caterers may spend hours—even days—planning the event with a client. Then once an event starts, the caterer becomes a ringmaster, coordinating everything that happens. Once it is over, the caterer begins planning the next event. How busy caterers are from day to day depends on how many events they have scheduled, while their income depends on such factors as the number and size of events scheduled, as well as their expertise and style.

Owner-operators of catering firms may make as much as $80,000 a year, with well-known and popular caterers earning even more. Most caterers who start their own businesses learn the trade by working for other caterers and in restaurants or hotels with catering services.

A Popular Caterer

Since 1981, Cynthia Davis Catering has been doing custom catering and event planning. The company is known for its artistic and elegant culinary presentations and features the freshest of seasonal foods. Absolutely every food item is prepared by the catering firm—most at the site of the event. The company was founded by Cynthia Davis and is now being operated by her daughter, Monique, who learned the business by working with her mother.

Having an abundance of energy is an absolute prerequisite in operating a catering business. Monique is an extremely vivacious individual whose enthusiasm for planning parties totally enchants her clients. The majority of her events (weddings, dinner parties, cocktail parties, box lunches) are for fifty to one hundred people. However, she has imaginatively created events such as a lunch for two on a mountaintop. Working with Monique on events is a staff of people who are as upbeat and friendly as she is. She uses one staff member and a bartender for every twenty guests.

Handling a Party for Fifty. Planning an event begins with a consultation between Monique and the host. Typically, a contract changes five or six times until all details are finalized.

Besides providing the food and beverage, Monique's firm provides flowers, linens, chairs, and tables. Details such as the color of the napkins must be decided upon for certain events. All of this takes time.

Before the day of the event, Monique must arrange the staffing, rent any necessary supplies, and obtain the food she will need. On the day of the event, she makes the appetizers at home. Monique does all the other cooking at the event site with the help of her staff, except for pastries, which are made by her grandmother.

Here's a list of all the tasks that Monique completes on the day of an event:

- Loads the van with all necessary supplies, from food and flowers to tables
- Unloads the van at the event site
- Sets up the buffet table while the staff sets the tables and the bartender arranges the bar
- Puts final touches on the hors d'oeuvres
- Prepares the dinner while staff serves hors d'oeuvres (she may have a staff member help with preparation)
- Clears plates and glasses and replenishes the buffet along with her staff
- Washes all dishes and silverware, takes down tables, and cleans up with help of staff
- Reloads the van and departs for home

An event for fifty people requires a minimum of seven hours on site. When Monique leaves the event, she frequently receives appreciative hugs from her clients.

What It Takes to Be a Caterer. According to Monique, you must have a good understanding of the business side of catering, which includes setting costs, operating a computer, and writing contracts. You must be an outstanding cook who understands quantity cooking. Finally, to handle all the elements from office work to cooking to serving to cleaning and setting up an event, it is essential to be a person who has a great capacity for action.

For More Information

You can get a head start on a career in food service by taking an entry-level position in a restaurant. This will give you a solid idea of whether or not this is the career area for you.

Learn more about food-service careers and obtain directories of two- and four-year colleges offering courses or programs to prepare for food-service careers by writing to these associations:

National Restaurant Association Educational Foundation
175 West Jackson Boulevard, Suite 1500
Chicago, IL 60604
www.nraef.org

National Restaurant Association
1200 Seventeenth Street NW
Washington, DC 20036
www.restaurant.org

International Association of Culinary Professionals (IACP)
304 West Liberty Street, Suite 201
Louisville, KY 40202
www.iacp.com

National Association of Catering Executives
9881 Broken Land Parkway, Suite 101
Columbia, MD 21046
www.nace.net

Letters, Packages, and Parcels

Careers in Delivery Services

lanes roar in from the sky and trucks loaded with thousands of letters and packages race into the terminal. Hundreds of workers rush here and there moving freight, sorting cargo, and loading it on the planes and trucks that will take it to its destination. Individuals, businesses, and governments depend on delivery services to ship letters, packages, and parcels quickly—sometimes within a matter of hours. Every day millions of items are shipped all over the world. The key to successful delivery services is speed. In 1860, with the inauguration of the Pony Express, mail could be delivered between St. Joseph, Missouri, and San Francisco, California, in eight or nine days. Today letters and packages can be delivered across even greater distances overnight, and companies continue to try to move the mail even faster.

A career with a delivery service is a most appropriate choice for those who want jobs that demand fast and continuous action. There are jobs with the United States Postal Service, giant express transportation companies such as FedEx, DHL, and UPS, as well as regional and local delivery and messenger services. High-energy types in this career could find themselves peddling a bike on Wall Street, driving a delivery truck, walking a mail route, or flying between distant locations.

71

The U.S. Postal Service

Each day the U.S. Postal Service receives, sorts, and delivers millions of letters, bills, advertisements, magazines, and packages. To do this, it employs more than 750,000 workers, making it the largest employer of delivery-service workers in the United States. About 60 percent of these workers are either postal clerks, who sort mail and serve customers, or mail carriers, who deliver the mail. Visit a busy post office, and you will observe that the clerk behind the counter usually serves one customer after another. There may even be a line of people waiting to be served. This job requires an individual with the capacity to work quickly and at the same time be tactful and courteous in dealing with the public.

If you become a mail carrier, your job may start as early as 4:00 A.M. if you have a route in the business district. No matter where your route is, you will first spend some time in the post office sorting the mail for your route. Automation, however, has reduced and is continuing to reduce sorting time, allowing carriers to spend more time delivering mail.

If you become a mail handler, you will unload sacks of incoming mail; separate letters, parcel post, magazines, and newspapers; and transport these to the proper sorting and processing areas. You may also load mail into automated letter-sorting machines, perform postage-canceling operations, and rewrap packages damaged in processing. Any of these jobs can be physically demanding, as you are always on your feet moving mail in some way. It can also be stressful, as postal workers are being asked to process and deliver ever-larger quantities of mail under tight production deadlines and quotas. Furthermore, in times of high mail volume, you will be expected to work overtime.

Job Requirements and Training

There is keen competition for jobs, as postal workers receive attractive salaries and benefits and need to meet only modest educational requirements. To become eligible for a job, applicants have to take a test that measures speed and accuracy at checking names and numbers and ability to memorize mail distribution procedures. They also have to pass a physical examination. Applicants' names are then placed on a list according to their examination scores to be considered in order when a vacancy occurs. It usually takes one to two years after taking the test to be considered for a vacancy. Experienced workers train newly hired workers, who receive more training when new equipment or procedures are introduced.

A Mail Carrier

Selina Brunswig delivers mail in a suburban area that features widely spaced homes perched on hills as well as on level ground. It is a rather solitary route. Selina drives a small half-ton truck and has to be extremely cautious because the roads are narrow and the hills are steep. Selina has been a city carrier for nine years—all on the same route.

Selina started her career with the postal service working as a scheme clerk in a general mail facility. Scheme clerks have the task of keying a code on every letter that passes by them so that it can be routed correctly. Besides being able to work fast, she had to have a good memory. Selina had to glance at a letter and then instantly decide whether to designate it as state mail, foreign mail, military mail, San Francisco mail, or mail for another San Francisco Bay Area city. She worked from midnight to 8:30 A.M. in this job for several years until she became a mail carrier.

As a carrier, Selina works an eight-hour day. She starts her job at 7:15 A.M. after checking in on a computerized job clock. Then she picks up her keys and goes out to inspect her vehicle for any possible problems. Next, it's back to the post office to spend close to three hours sorting mail into cases in the exact order of her route. Because she has a high-volume route, Selina sorts from ten to fourteen feet of letters and flats (magazines and manila envelopes). Every letter must be placed in the correct spot in one of the cases that will go in her truck. Selina also has to indicate the addresses along the designated route where she will be dropping off packages.

Once all the sorting is completed, and it does have to be done rapidly, Selina puts all the mail and packages in a hamper and rolls them out to her truck and loads it. Then it's time to drive out to her route and begin delivering the mail. At each stop, she fingers through several cases to be sure she has all the letters, magazines, advertisements, and packages for that address. Selina has developed a system for this work that enables her to deliver the mail quickly. (Each carrier devises a system that works the easiest for him or her.) Frequently, this busy carrier has to jump out of the truck to leave a package at the door. Also, she takes the time to provide extra services for a few of the elderly people on her route. When she has completed her route, Selina returns to the post office. If she has not worked eight hours, she usually sorts and cases bulk mail until she has.

Selina is pleased that she has stayed on the same route for so many years. She knows so many of the people on the route and finds them to be polite and friendly. She finds being a mail carrier an ideal job for a peppy person and plans to be delivering mail for many years.

A Look at Large Express Transportation Companies

When you begin to describe large express transportation companies that offer service worldwide, you are dealing with huge numbers. These companies deliver millions of packages every day, employ tens of thousands of workers, have hundreds of aircraft and thousands of vehicles, and have hundreds of facilities scattered across the country and even the world. The one thing that all these companies have in common is fast service. This means jobs for those who like the challenge of working every day at "warp" speed. Speed is especially important in jobs involving the pickup, sorting, and delivery of packages. All of these companies also have large office staffs.

FedEx offers its customers service when it "absolutely, positively" has to be there. Overnight service is available that brings items to customers as early as the next business morning. The speed of international service varies by location. Every business day, FedEx delivers more than 5.4 million items to over two hundred countries. It delivers packages of virtually any size and weight. The company employs more than 218,000 people throughout the world, operates 640 aircraft and more than 70,000 vehicles, and has more than 41,000 customer convenience locations worldwide.

UPS was founded in 1907 in Seattle, Washington. From its small beginnings, it has grown into a company that transports more than 3.4 billion parcels and documents each year throughout the world with a staff of approximately 360,000 people. With its global service, UPS can actually reach more than four billion people, which is double the number of people who can be reached by any telephone. The company is primarily owned by its management and employees and is the world's largest package distribution company.

DHL Global offers desk-to-desk service to virtually every business center in the world. The company serves almost every city in 223 countries around the world and has more than 150,000 employees. On an average day, more than one million DHL shipments are sent to destinations throughout the world. DHL operates seventy-eight hubs worldwide where packages and letters are unloaded, sorted, reloaded aboard aircraft, and then flown to their destination cities.

A FedEx Driver

After graduation from high school, Thomas King got a job with FedEx unloading planes at a hub airport. He worked between

10:00 P.M. and 2:00 A.M. and was able to attend college full-time because of his work schedule and the company's tuition reimbursement plan. Before Thomas graduated from college, he had worked his way up to a supervisory position directing employees in the off-loading and on-loading of planes. After Thomas graduated from college, he decided he wanted to keep working at FedEx and applied for a position as a route driver. To qualify for this position, you have to be twenty-one years old and have a very good driving record. Typically, individuals have to work in other company jobs before becoming a driver.

Today, Thomas drives a FedEx truck on a residential route in a suburban area. He works at one of the five largest stations the company has. From the moment he clocks in at 6:30 A.M. until the time he quits around 3:30 P.M., he is on the go. He begins his workday by getting a tracker, a handheld computer, which he initializes for his route and the company's computer system. Then he checks the oil level and lights of his truck and inspects it for any problems. Next, he goes to a very long belt that is being filled with packages from semi trucks. The packages move slowly down the belt, traveling one-half mile in a minute. Thomas stands in a sort position on the belt and pulls off packages for three routes. The truck for each route is behind him. Thomas has memorized all the streets on these routes. He has to look at the label on each package that goes by him on the belt to see if it belongs on one of his routes. When he finds a package for one of his routes, he lifts it off the belt and places it in the right truck. You definitely need to be in good shape to handle this job. This sorting of packages is not completed until approximately 8:15 A.M.

On the Route. When Thomas is ready to start his route, he turns the computer on in his truck and signs in. He uses the computer along the way to communicate with the company and to learn of any pickups that he should make. Aboard his truck, he usually has approximately one hundred items to deliver. (A driver on a business or industrial route would have more pieces, as multiple items are frequently left at each delivery stop.) Thomas concentrates on delivering the priority overnight shipments first, as they are guaranteed to arrive at their destination by 10:30 A.M. These shipments have been placed on a separate shelf in the truck.

The same procedure is followed for each package. Thomas checks if the recipient has a signature release on file. The next step is to enter into the tracker the signature release number, street, and street number and to scan the bar code. The tracker is then placed in the computer that sends all this information about the package to the central hub in Memphis, Tennessee. Customers then can use the Internet to find out exactly when their packages were delivered.

After 10:30 A.M., Thomas begins to do regular pickups as well as call-in pickups along with delivering items to customers. When he picks up a letter or package, he always enters the zip code and first letter of the city where it is going into the computer. A printed label emerges from the onboard printer and is placed on the letter or package. This is the routing instruction that will be used throughout the journey of the package. Thomas's day on the job is not over until every item on the truck is delivered. On days with an extra large number of items and no extra help, he may work as long as twelve hours. At the end of the day, he returns to the station, where the truck is unloaded by other workers and prepared for the next day's work.

Besides handling his duties as a driver, Thomas has the additional responsibility of serving as a trainer. This involves taking newly hired drivers on his route and showing them how he does the job. After this training session, the new drivers go to a two-week courier school for formal training.

Thomas believes that his job is a perfect one for people who like to be in shape and stay active and on top of things all day long. His job could lead to a management position supervising other drivers at this station or another station.

Local Delivery Services

It isn't just the big, well-known companies that deliver letters and packages. Most cities have a number of small companies offering delivery services. The services may be confined to a city or extend throughout an area or even a state. These companies offer both same-day and overnight delivery service. Some promise to deliver in a hurry anything from a letter to a truckload. Many have overnight and daily route deliveries, while a few offer additional services such as crating and storage. These companies have opportunities for both full-time and part-time employment for those who like to rush around.

A Locally Owned Delivery Service

The goal of Bay Area Delivery in Concord, California, is to foster dependability and confidence with the deliveries. The company offers immediate service, same-day service, and airport service as well as overnight service. It delivers items that weigh from one pound to ten thousand pounds in an area extending from the state capital in Sacramento to San Jose in the heart of Silicon Valley (a distance of about 125 miles).

The company's work primarily focuses on the delivery of packages. Many of its customers are major high-tech companies, where packages are picked up and then delivered to local customers or taken to the airport. Delivery work can be exciting, especially when there is a medical emergency and the company has to pick up a part for a CAT scanner and rush it to the airport to catch a certain flight. Of course, every day there is last-minute work, especially from graphic artists who want to get their work to customers by the end of the business day.

Robert and Pat Clarenbach own Bay Area Delivery. They work in the office eight to ten hours a day dispatching drivers and handling the paperwork. This is an on-time, on-call business that operates around the clock, 365 days a year. When the Clarenbachs leave the office, the business goes with them, as the phone rings in their home. The busiest time of day for them is between 8:00 A.M. and 2:00 P.M., as 90 percent of the calls come in during this time. Then there is a minirush of calls between 3:30 P.M. and 5:00 P.M. each afternoon.

When a call comes in, one of the Clarenbachs answers it, writes down the delivery details, and dispatches a driver to the location for the pickup. The Clarenbachs communicate with their drivers by pagers, phones, and two-way radios. A few of the approximately ten drivers hang around the office waiting for assignments, but most are at home or in their own cars or company trucks handling deliveries or waiting for another job assignment. Four of the drivers start at 6:00 A.M. and travel a regular route, picking up packages and delivering them to customers or to the airport. Then, like the other drivers, they are on call for the rest of the day. At times, business is so brisk that Robert has to go out and do pickups and deliveries. Usually, he is able to find part-time drivers when they are extremely busy. According to Robert, you need to be a high-energy person to handle this job because the focus is always on rushing.

Recently, the Clarenbachs began to expand into warehousing. They plan to store records of businesses and professionals such as doctors and lawyers. They pick up and keep the records as well as return records as requested. Their son, Scott, who has joined the company, will concentrate on this operation. Right now, Scott serves as a backup dispatcher, drives the truck when heavy deliveries are needed, and handles some pickups and deliveries. He spends two days a week delivering treadmills that are stored in the warehouse to customers who have purchased them from exercise equipment stores. Like his parents, Scott finds the delivery business to be one in which there is always something to do.

Messengers

A messenger literally needs to travel as fast as possible for the simple reason that senders may want an item to reach its destination within an hour. They pick up and deliver letters, important business documents, or packages that need to be sent or received in a hurry within a local area. Messengers work in large cities and often use bicycles or mopeds in congested areas such as Wall Street, which can be hazardous because of the heavy traffic. Their work hours usually parallel those of businesses, but a few work nights and on weekends.

Messengers receive their instructions either by reporting to the office in person or by telephone, beeper, or two-way radio. After a delivery is completed, they check with the office and receive instructions about the next delivery. They usually maintain records of deliveries and often obtain signatures from the persons receiving the items. You can find a job as a messenger with messenger companies or businesses such as banks and law offices that have important documents they want delivered quickly.

Job Qualifications and Earnings

Being a messenger is often a first job, as there aren't any formal qualifications. If you decide to become a messenger, you need to have a good geographic knowledge of the area in which you travel as well as a good sense of direction. You need to be in good physical condition if you become a bicycle messenger and to have a driver's license and a good driving record if you are using a car. Expect to earn between $250 and $515 a week, and you may also get occasional tips.

A Look at the Future

With the increasing emphasis on the speed of deliveries, high-energy people will continue to find jobs with the postal service, express transportation companies, and local delivery services. Job growth with the postal service will slow, however, because of the growing popularity of new forms of electronic communication. The number of messenger jobs is declining because technology has brought so many other ways, such as faxes and e-mail, that businesses can use to communicate with each other. Messengers will still be needed, however, to transport materials such as blueprints and legal documents that cannot be sent electronically.

For More Information

Additional information about job opportunities for messengers may be obtained from local employers and local offices of the state employment service. Besides working for messenger services, messengers can find jobs with mail-order firms, banks, printing and publishing firms, utility companies, retail stores, and other large firms.

For information about employment as a mail carrier or with a package-delivery service, visit these websites:

United States Postal Service: www.usps.com
FedEx: www.fedex.com
UPS: www.ups.com
DHL Global: www.dhl.com

CHAPTER SEVEN

Dance, Act, and Direct

Careers in Entertainment

You see them in the entertainment spotlight all the time: Television and movie actors performing in fast-moving, exciting shows. Singers and their bands entertaining thousands of people at concerts, their tours often visiting many cities throughout the United States. Broadway actors performing to sold-out crowds night after night.

These performers have careers that require a very high level of energy. The people behind the scenes who manage performers and direct and produce concerts, shows, movies, and television programs are also high-energy people. The entertainment industry is one that demands people to be vibrant, spirited, and full of vigor, for it is a fast-moving world with a need to produce new entertainment constantly.

Dancers

Whether you dance in a classical ballet, modern dance group, musical show, music video, movie, television show, or opera, dancing is strenuous. There are always long hours of rehearsals and rigorous practice sessions. And when dancers are part of shows, they perform evenings and weekends and may be traveling from city to city. Furthermore, to become a professional dancer, years of intensive training are required, whether you will be dancing in music videos or with a major ballet company. Dancers need good health and physical stamina to follow the demanding schedule required of them.

Training to Become a Dancer

No matter what type of dancer you become, training is absolutely essential, and more than likely you will need to begin training when you are quite young. More training is required for ballet than any other form of dance. Women may begin training before they are in elementary school to become ballerinas, with serious training beginning between the ages of ten and twelve. Men are more likely to begin ballet training between the ages of ten and fifteen. Then in their early teens, those who demonstrate potential will receive more intensive and advanced training at regional ballet schools or schools associated with major ballet companies. Leading dance school companies often have summer training programs from which they select candidates for their regular full-time training programs. Most ballet dancers have their professional auditions by age seventeen or eighteen.

A college education is definitely not essential to obtaining employment as a professional dancer, but it is helpful for those who retire early and become dance teachers and choreographers.

Career Overview

If you plan to become a dancer, you can expect to face intense competition for jobs. Besides, to get most jobs you need to audition. You also need to realize that only the most talented dancers will find regular employment. Careers do tend to be short in dance, as most people stop performing in their late thirties, with only a few celebrated dancers performing after they are fifty. Many dancers do continue, however, to work in the field as choreographers, dance teachers, coaches, and artistic directors.

Expect to join a union if you are a professional dancer in a major ballet or modern dance company, a musical or Broadway show, a movie, or a TV show. This will only govern the minimum amount of money that you earn—you could earn more. Professional dancers have an average annual salary of about $25,200. A principal may earn $1,000 or more a week. Dancers in film musicals usually earn around $120 per day of filming.

A Dancer with the San Francisco Ballet

The San Francisco Ballet is regarded as one of the finest ballet companies in the United States. The story of one of the young dancers in this company will show you very clearly just how strenuous this career is, with long hours devoted to practice and rehearsals.

Jennifer Blake begged her family for dance lessons for several years before she began taking ballet lessons when she was eight. It was an immediate love affair, and within a year, she was taking lessons three times a week, and then five. By the time Jennifer was in high school, she was singing and dancing in shows like "Sweet Charity" and devoting from one and a half to three hours a day to intense practice, rehearsals, and dance lessons (ballet, tap, jazz). Besides taking dance lessons in her hometown during the school year, Jennifer attended summer sessions at the San Francisco Ballet School and several other ballet companies. It was not until she was fifteen, however, that Jennifer decided to focus on ballet, which is late to make this type of career decision.

Attending Ballet School. After graduating from high school, Jennifer auditioned and was accepted into the summer program at the San Francisco Ballet School. The intensive six-week program included classes in ballet technique, character dancing, and music theory. After the conclusion of the summer session, Jennifer received a full scholarship to attend the ballet school. For two years, she worked intensely for up to six and seven hours a day at the school perfecting her skills so that she could become a member of the corps de ballet of the San Francisco Ballet. It is important to understand that the competition for a position with this company is very keen. While in the ballet school, Jennifer also began to perform with the ballet company, which was rather like a tryout to see how she would perform with the other dancers. Her efforts were rewarded with an apprenticeship (a trial year) in the company. Then she was selected to become a member of the corps de ballet in 1992.

Life in the Corps de Ballet. During the performance season, from late November to the end of May, Jennifer works six days a week. After each ballet program, which lasts a month, there is a three-week rehearsal period. Rehearsal days are rather busy. They start at approximately ten o'clock in the morning with a ninety-minute ballet class that includes warming up, stretching, and basic steps. After lunch, time is spent rehearsing the next ballets with approximately one hour devoted to each ballet. Typically, rehearsal days end at 6:30 or 7:00 P.M. Performance days are far busier for Jennifer. First, there are up to four hours of rehearsals, which end by five o'clock. Then after a short dinner break, Jennifer returns to the theater to stretch and warm up, dress, and do her hair and makeup before performing in the ballet.

Jennifer cannot imagine another career and would love to stay with San Francisco Ballet. She works on a yearly contract, and staying with the company depends on an annual evaluation. Jennifer's career looks quite promising, as she has already danced some principal and soloist roles in both contemporary and classical ballets.

Musicians

Performing music takes energy, whether you are conducting a symphony orchestra, playing an instrument in a band, or singing country ballads. It also takes musical talent; however, talent alone is no guarantee of success. You need to have dedication, self-discipline, and drive to rise to the top. Musicians also have to have physical stamina: you can see this when you watch the dance moves of singers in their videos, the swift bowing of violinists in symphony orchestras, and the drumming of drummers in bands.

Career Opportunities for Musicians

The glamour and potentially high earnings of careers in music attract many talented individuals. Unfortunately, many musicians find only part-time work or experience bouts of unemployment between engagements and decide they cannot support themselves as musicians. Often, they take permanent full-time jobs in other occupations, while working only part-time as musicians. Still, more than a quarter of a million people hold jobs as musicians.

If you are a classical musician, you may find a job with a major or regional symphony orchestra, an opera company, a ballet or theater production, or a small quartet or trio. If you are a popular musician, you'll find jobs in clubs, restaurants, and theaters, as well as for private events. And if you become well known, you will find yourself giving concerts, appearing on radio and television, making recordings and videos, and going on concert tours. Dreams of a musical future can come true; you could be the next world-renowned symphony conductor or singing sensation.

Is Formal Training Necessary?

Classical musicians, whether they play instruments, conduct orchestras, or sing, require years of formal training in order to acquire the necessary skill, knowledge, and ability to interpret music. Most begin studying music when they are very young. Not only will they study with accomplished musicians, they may also attend a music conservatory or participate in a college or university music program. On the other hand, popular musicians may have little formal training.

Becoming a Performer

Just like dancers, classical musicians have to audition in order to get jobs performing with opera companies, orchestras, choirs, or theatrical productions. They typically start with small companies and advance to better-known groups as their skills increase. Quite often, popular musicians begin their careers by playing or singing without pay at clubs and community and social functions. Then they advance to paying jobs as their audience grows and more people begin to like their music. If their music becomes truly popular, they may get recording contracts and be on their way to a blockbuster career.

A Rock Musician

Dave Carter has been a professional musician since he was in high school in the sixties. A fellow student taught him to play the bass, and his career was off and running. Soon he was one of the four members of the Virtues, playing at local high school dances. Bill Graham, who had a very big reputation in San Francisco as a promoter at that time, saw the young group playing in a local park and said he would like to have them start his shows.

Soon they were opening shows for such legends as Janis Joplin and the Grateful Dead and had changed the group's name to Country Weather at Graham's request, even though they played rock 'n' roll. Their performances sizzled with energy as they played and sang. At a typical performance, they would play two sets of forty-five minutes each as well as a couple of encores. To keep playing at such a high level, they would rehearse four nights a week for three hours.

In the course of the eight years the group was together, they played with performers such as Ike and Tina Turner, Credence Clearwater, Eric Clapton, and Santana. The band members all started college but dropped out after two years because they were playing so much and getting the attention to move to recording. Unfortunately, their manager had a disagreement with Graham, which ended their getting big jobs, and the band broke up.

Dave then started his own band that he called D.C. Rush. At first, the band played in clubs in the Lake Tahoe area; however, today Dave concentrates on playing for private parties in the San Francisco Bay Area. Now tapes that the original band made in the sixties have been turned into CDs and are being sold in record stores. Dave has been fortunate to have a long career in music.

The Magic of Actors, Directors, and Producers

Actors, directors, and producers bring the words of a script to life on the stage, movie screens, radio, and television. Without question, there are many people aspiring to follow in the footsteps of famous actors and directors like Tom Cruise, Julia Roberts, Sofia Coppola, and Steven Spielberg.

Fortunately, future employment opportunities have increased for all people desiring these careers. There is a rising domestic demand for entertainment—fueled by the growth of cable television, home movie rentals, and television syndications as well as increased foreign demand for American productions. This growth of opportunity in film and television productions should be accompanied by an increasing number of jobs in live productions. Furthermore, touring productions of Broadway plays and other large shows are providing more jobs for actors and directors. Even with employment opportunities growing, competition for jobs as actors, directors, and producers will remain intense, and only the most talented will find regular employment.

Where the Jobs Are

New York City is decidedly the place with the most job opportunities if you want to be in a theatrical production, and it is also where casts are normally selected for shows that go on the road. Nevertheless, there are many solid employment opportunities in all major cities, as well as in smaller regional theaters. Many cities have small professional companies such as little theaters, repertory companies, and dinner theaters, which provide opportunities for local amateur talent as well as for professional entertainers. In addition, job seekers should check out summer theaters in resort and suburban areas, on cruise ships, and in amusement parks.

If you want to work in the movies, Hollywood and New York City are the centers for these activities. However, studios are also located in Florida, Seattle, and many other cities. Television opportunities abound at the network entertainment centers in New York and Los Angeles and at local television stations around the country.

Getting Started in the Entertainment Arena

Experience counts in the entertainment industry. Aspiring actors and directors should take part in high school and college plays or work with little theaters and other acting groups. Then they can build on these experiences to get bigger jobs. Formal dramatic training in theater, arts, and dramatic literature and from college courses and dramatic arts schools can be helpful, too, in obtaining jobs. For example, David Hyde-Pierce, who played Frasier's brother Niles on television, studied drama at Yale University, and actor Dean Cain was in theater productions at Princeton University. As the reputations of actors, directors, and producers grow, they work on larger productions or in more prestigious roles. Actors also advance to lead or specialized roles.

A Realistic Look at Earnings

The salaries of actors and directors can be fabulous, and they often include a percentage of a show's earnings or ticket sales. You have probably read or heard that actors and actresses like Adam Sandler and Cameron Diaz earned more than $40 million dollars a year for their acting. It is a false impression that all actors are highly paid. The Screen Actors Guild reports that the average income its members earned from acting was less than $5,000 per year. This means that many actors must supplement their incomes with other jobs.

While the minimum weekly salary for a Broadway stage production is $1,250, a small, off-Broadway production's minimum ranges from $440 to $728 a week, depending on the number of seats in the theater. Motion picture and television actors with speaking parts receive a minimum daily rate of $636, or $2,206 for a five-day week. Those without speaking parts, or "extras," earn a minimum rate of about $115 per day. Actors also receive additional compensation when shows that they are in are sold into syndication; they get paid every time a show is rerun. These "residuals" can mean that an actor is still getting paid for work he or she did twenty years ago.

The income of stage directors varies greatly. Summer theaters offer compensation ranging from $2,500 to $8,000 for a three- to four-week run of a production. Regional theaters often hire directors for longer periods of time, so their compensation is greater. The highest-paid stage directors typically can earn more than $87,700 plus royalties for a production. Producers of stage shows seldom receive a set fee; instead, they receive a percentage of a show's earnings or ticket sales. The earnings of movie directors vary with their reputations and frequently include a percentage of what the movies earn.

Working as an Actor with a Professional Theater Company

Only a few actors ever achieve worldwide recognition as actors on the stage, in motion pictures, or on television. However, through more than twenty years of work at the Center Repertory Company in Walnut Creek, California, Kerri Shawn has built a solid reputation as a regional theater actress. It all started when Kerri, a shy high school student, was called upon to read a poem in her English class. Her teacher saw a "spark" in her performance and suggested that Kerri try out for the school play. She auditioned, won the part, was promptly bitten by the acting bug, and has been acting ever since. Kerri prepared for her career by majoring in theater in college and is still taking classes and workshops to refine her acting skills. After college, she began working with Center Repertory Company. Her first role was Stella in A Streetcar Named Desire. Since then, she has been cast in one to three roles a year in parts ranging from comedy to drama. Kerri has played such parts as Kate in *The Taming of the Shrew*, Lady Macduff in *Macbeth*, and Edna in *The Prisoner of Second Avenue*. Occasionally, she sings as part of a role; however, she is not a trained singer.

On the Job. Each play is a ten- to twelve-week commitment for Kerri, with the first four to six weeks devoted to rehearsals. This means rehearsing Tuesday through Sunday from 7:00 to 10:30 P.M., on Saturday from 10:00 A.M. to 6:00 P.M., and on Sunday from noon until 6:00 P.M. Typically, she is one of the few locals in the production, which frequently has well-known guest artists, such as Jonathan McMurtry of the Old Globe Theater, who was brought in for a Shakespearian play. Each play runs for five weeks with performances Wednesday through Sunday.

Another continuing acting project for Kerri is performing with the Fantasy Forum Actors Ensemble. This group produces family entertainment in the form of one-hour musicals. They do productions of fairy tales such as *Hansel and Gretel* and *Cinderella*. Before the show, the actors talk from the stage to the audience, and after the show the children are able to shake hands with the costumed actors. Because acting is her passion, Kerri also plays roles in other nearby theaters and does many industrial films.

Kerri feels fortunate to work as an actor in her community. She is especially pleased that quality work is always available in the Northern California area where she lives. In the future, as her children grow up, she sees herself venturing out beyond the community for acting work.

A Young Hollywood Director

Christian Ford wants to direct films. He wrote and directed *Slow Burn*. For the leads in his movie he cast Minnie Driver, James Spader, and Josh Brolin. *Slow Burn* is a thriller revolving around three people trapped in an unforgiving desert with a broken truck, a locked box of diamonds, and four days of water. It was shot entirely on location in the desert.

Since his graduation from college with a major in film, Christian has been busy writing screenplays with the idea of creating one that he could direct. This is the way that young directors are getting started in the film industry today. Christian is well prepared for this career, as he has directed some commercials and music videos. He has also become totally familiar with all the technical skills involved in movie making through work as a cameraman, electrician, sound recordist, and sound mixer. And perhaps most importantly, he has refined his communication skills, since the director must orchestrate a crew of at least thirty people in addition to the actors.

As the director of a film, Christian will have a vision of the complete movie in his head. When a scene is to be shot, he will be able to tell the actors exactly how it fits into the plot and what emotions they should be feeling. This is essential because movies are not usually shot in chronological order. He will also be able to describe for the crew the most minute details of the scene—even the color of the paint on the walls.

Directing a movie is a very time-sensitive activity because so much must be accomplished in a short time. The crew and the actors must be prepared for a scene, it has to be rehearsed, then shot, and then it's time to set up for the next scene. This is repeated throughout the long days of shooting, which last at least twelve hours. Directing is also a physically taxing career with the long hours and frequently arduous environments. For example, Christian directed his film in the desert in July.

A director's job is not confined to the shooting of a film. Most movie shoots last between four and thirty weeks; however, for the director, the entire process takes about a year for smaller movies and two years for larger movies. Christian was actively involved in casting the movie. He also was busy creating the storyboards for the film. A storyboard is like a comic book of the movie; it shows what almost every scene of the film will look like. Not all directors do the storyboards themselves, but Christian was very concerned with the visual aspect of his film. After the film was shot, Christian worked with the editors, sound effects editors, composers, and musicians to complete the creation of the movie he envisioned. After this movie's release, he hopes to be established in Hollywood as a director and find it easier to be hired, as he will have shown what he can do. Christian hopes to be able to continue directing movies of value.

A Hollywood Success Story

If you saw the movie *Groundhog Day*, starring Bill Murray and Andie McDowell, then you have seen a movie in which Whitney White played a prominent role as associate producer. Perhaps, instead, you have seen *Multiplicity*, starring Michael Keaton; Whitney was the coproducer of this film. Just twelve short years after her graduation from UCLA with a major in film and television, Whitney is rapidly climbing the film production career ladder. Her Hollywood career was launched during her senior year in college when she served an internship as a production assistant with Ocean Pictures. In this job, she did anything and everything required on the set, from answering phones to picking up lunch for the crew. Whitney's enthusiasm and unflagging energy on the set led to a paying job with the company after her graduation.

At first, Whitney worked fifty- to sixty-hour weeks as a production assistant. When the film was finished, she became a postproduction assistant and learned this phase of the business, which includes such things as getting the credits in order and setting up screenings. Her next step up the film production career ladder was to become the assistant to the owners of Ocean Pictures. In this job, she learned about the development of film properties. After a stint as an associate producer, Whitney became a coproducer of Ocean Pictures' films and vice president of development.

Whitney's Responsibilities. When Whitney works as vice president of development, she is in the office searching for new projects. This means reading scripts, looking at books and magazines, and talking to authors with the hope of finding the perfect property to film. Once a script is chosen, Whitney works with the producers for a year or more to get it ready for filming. It takes constant feedback between the writers, producers, and studio to get a film project the way all these different people want it to appear. At the same time, Whitney continues searching for more projects.

Once a film is in production, Whitney's role changes to coproducer and her major job is to make the film happen. On *Multiplicity*, this meant serving as the liaison between the production company and the special effects company that was creating effects that had never been done before. Whitney also hired crew, talked budget with the studio, worked with the marketing department, entertained actors, and prepared for the shoot. She served as the glue that held all the pieces together. It is a seven-day-a-week job that could only be held by a person like Whitney, who has boundless energy.

Some Jobs in Radio and Television

If you are on the air in radio and television giving the news or hosting a talk show, you have to be very focused on what you are doing, even though someone may be whispering instructions through your earpiece or holding up a sign for you to read. These are high-pressure jobs. Behind the scenes, high-energy people are needed to put these shows together and direct what is happening when the shows go on the air.

A Radio Talk Show Producer

Patty Stanton is producer of *The Ronn Owens Show*, which airs five mornings a week on KGO in San Francisco. This is a popular news talk show. Ronn, the host, interacts with the callers and also interviews guests. Producing this show is an action-packed job that begins before the show and continues after the show is over. Patty arrives at the radio station at 7:00 A.M. and immediately starts putting together a list of topics that Ronn may wish to discuss on the air that day. She swiftly scans three newspapers, looks at wire services on the computer, and goes through information faxes in her search for interesting topics. By the time Ronn arrives at 8:00, she has assembled a pile of ideas for him. Between 8:00 and 9:00, they discuss the day's program and prepare for the show.

The show is on the air between 9:00 and 11:45 A.M. This is a busy time. Patty screens the calls on eleven incoming lines, looking for callers who exhibit passion and have provocative views. At the same time, she is handling faxes from listeners to select those Ronn may wish to read on the air. She is also keeping an eye on CNN for late-breaking news. In addition, the engineer could be talking to her, or the station intercom could be announcing an upcoming ABC newsbreak. In the midst of all this, Patty is feeding information to Ronn, who is separated from her in a glass booth. They communicate by using hand signals, e-mail on their computers, and the station intercom.

Once the show is over, the pace slows; however, much still remains to be done before Patty leaves the station at three o'clock. She books people for future shows, reviews books to evaluate whether their authors should be guests, and fields phone calls from people who want to be on the show. Often, she takes production work home to do, which includes putting together music bumpers for the show. Bumpers are the musical clips that introduce, accompany, or close a radio or television segment.

Future Outlook

The entertainment industry is one of the fastest growing in the United States. The pressure to produce an ever-increasing number of TV shows, movies, records, and concerts means the employment of people in this industry will keep growing. High-energy people are needed to fuel this demand both as performers and behind-the-scenes workers.

For More Information

The organizations listed here can provide more helpful information about careers in the entertainment world.

DANCERS

National Dance Association
American Alliance for Health, Physical Education, Recreation, and Dance
1900 Association Drive
Reston, VA 20191
www.aahperd.org/nda

Professional Dancers Federation
6830 North Broadway "D"
Denver, CO 80221
www.pdfusa.org

MUSICIANS

American Guild of Musical Artists
1430 Broadway, Fourteenth Floor
New York, NY 10018
www.musicalartists.org

American Society of Composers, Authors, and Publishers
One Lincoln Plaza
New York, NY 10023
www.ascap.com

ACTORS, DIRECTORS, AND PRODUCERS

Actors' Equity Association
165 West Forty-Sixth Street
New York, NY 10036
www.actorsequity.org

American Federation of Television and Radio Artists
260 Madison Avenue
New York, NY 10016
www.aftra.org

Association of Independent Video and Filmmakers
304 Hudson Street, Sixth Floor
New York, NY 10013
www.aivf.org

Screen Actors Guild—Los Angeles
5757 Wilshire Boulevard
Los Angeles, CA 90036
www.sag.org

Screen Actors Guild—New York
360 Madison Avenue, Twelfth Floor
New York, NY 10017
www.sag.org

CHAPTER EIGHT

Sell, Buy, and Invest

Careers in the Business World

The business world moves at the speed of light. Businesses strive to provide the highest-quality products or services with the best customer service in the quickest time possible. The competition for business is fierce, but the rewards can be great. While some people work for a business, innovative individuals start their own business. Being an entrepreneur takes ambition, initiative, and energy. JCPenney, Ford, and Microsoft all started as small enterprises. You could be the next Bill Gates; every year, energetic go-getters like you start more than five hundred thousand new businesses.

Within the vast world of business, there are certain jobs that demand people to be alert, focused, and on their toes literally every minute of the day. They are not desk jobs—they're action jobs that often move at a frantic pace. Many require far more hours on the job than the traditional forty.

Sales: High-Energy People Needed

Computers, compact discs, clothing, automobiles, and thousands of other products are bought and sold each day. Manufacturers make products that sales representatives sell to retail establishments, government agencies, and other institutions. Then in turn sales clerks at retail firms sell the products to customers. Because the income of people in sales is often closely tied to how much they sell, they need to be ceaseless in their quest for sales, making this a perfect job for high-energy types. They also need these qualities to succeed:

- **Patience and perseverance**—because completing a sale may take months.
- **Physical stamina**—because they may be on their feet for long periods of time or have to carry heavy sample cases.
- **Persuasiveness**—because customers must often be convinced that a certain product is the best for their needs.
- **Goal-oriented personality**—because they may need to set personal sales goals or make company sales quotas.
- **Knowledge**—because customers will expect them to have solid product information, and the company will expect them to stay abreast of new products and changing consumer needs.
- **Pleasant personality**—because they will need to work well with customers.
- **Communication skills**—because they will need to explain the advantages of purchasing a product.

Sales Representatives

Sales representatives market their company's products, whether they are selling fabric to furniture makers, desks to government agencies, or books to schools. Whenever they are with customers, they must be vibrant and in the "sell" mode. They also need to be full of energy to handle all the traveling that they'll be doing. Some sales representatives have large territories covering several states or even foreign countries, requiring them to be away from home for several days or weeks at a time. Many sales representatives, however, work near the home base and do most of their traveling by automobile. Expect to work more than forty hours per week with all the travel involved as a sales representative, plus the need to visit a great number of customers. One big plus to this job is that you will probably have the freedom to determine your own schedule.

Job Requirements

You may not need to be a college graduate. Your sales ability, energetic personality, and familiarity with a product may be sufficient for many sales jobs, unless you are selling a product that requires specific technical knowledge. Most firms, however, are now placing greater emphasis on education for their sales representatives and will expect you to have a college degree. Do expect some on-the-job training, whether it is accompanying more experienced workers on their sales calls, taking training classes, or participating in a formal training program that could last up to two years.

Earnings

Sales representatives are usually paid a combination of salary and commission or salary plus bonus. In either case, the more energetic you are and the more sales you make, the higher your income will be. Most sales representatives earn between $37,400 and $74,600 a year. However, the top 10 percent earn more than $102,000 a year. How much you make depends on the type of goods or services you are selling. You can expect to be reimbursed for expenses such as transportation costs, meals, hotels, and entertaining customers, and you may have perks such as a company car and frequent flyer mileage.

A Successful Sales Representative

Nolan Lai projects enthusiasm for his job, his company, and his future. He sells arc-welding products as a technical sales representative for Lincoln Electric. Because he sells a product requiring technical expertise, Nolan spent almost a year in a formal company training program. All of the trainees were college graduates with engineering degrees. Besides classes to learn about the company and its products, Nolan spent a couple of months learning how to weld—an essential skill for anyone selling welding products. He also spent time surveying the company's plant to find ways that manufacturing costs could be reduced because as a salesperson he would be looking for ways other companies could reduce costs by using his company's products or by changing the way they operate. Once Nolan was assigned to a sales territory, he went with other salespeople in the office on joint sales calls for about two weeks before he began to work his own territory.

All in a Day's Work. Nolan is a high-energy person who is on the go from as early as 5:30 A.M. to as late as 10:00 or 11:00 P.M. He travels from twenty-eight hundred to twenty-nine hundred miles in a month on business because he has a large territory. In a typical day, he visits two or three distributors who sell his company's products to end users. He needs to persuade them of the advantages of continuing to sell the products, plus tell them about any technological advances that have been made in the product or in using the product. He also visits three or four end users to let them know they can come to him for technical advice. He may also make some cold calls.

Nolan's focus is always on making more sales. Some days he may be in a suit talking to top management. On others, you may find him in jeans on top of a bridge demonstrating how to make a certain weld. At other times, he is giving training classes at a customer's plant or job site on how to use his company's products or how to handle certain welding procedures.

An extremely important part of his sales effort is making sure that everyone knows how to use his company's products, as well as showing companies how to save money by using certain procedures and products. Before a workday ever starts or after it is over, Nolan has paperwork to do. The job does not have much downtime. While he travels between customers, he is constantly returning calls on his car phone and receiving messages on his beeper. Every week or ten days, he spends a day at the office handling his current sales efforts, making new sales contacts, and fielding calls from customers regarding the company's product line.

Climbing the Career Ladder. In Nolan's firm, the typical career ladder for a sales representative involves advancing to a larger territory, a higher-profile office, or a suboffice where he or she is the only salesperson. The next step would be to district sales management. However, Nolan will bypass the usual process and become project manager for North America, reporting to the national sales manager and company president. In his new job, he will travel throughout the United States and Canada, taking on various projects as he looks for ways to expand sales.

Real Estate Sales

Commissions on sales are the major source of income for the real estate agent—few receive a salary. The more homes they sell, the more agents will earn. So being an energetic person with the capacity to work evenings and weekends as well as during the workday is absolutely essential. It is also important to be able to juggle many tasks throughout the workday, from closing deals to showing homes to finding new homes to list. The sales process begins when the real estate salesperson meets with clients to get a feeling for the type of home they would like and can afford. Then clients are taken to see a number of homes that are likely to meet their needs and income. Bargaining may be necessary to get the best possible price. Once the sales contract has been signed by both parties, the agent must see to it that all special terms of the contract are upheld, from having radon and termite inspections to making sure the homeowner has repainted the front door. On the other side, when real estate salespeople list a property for sale, they must work with the client to present the property in the best possible way, develop a sales strategy, and set a sales price.

While real estate agents are not required to have a college education, they must hold a state license, which typically requires completing between thirty and ninety hours of classroom instruction and passing a comprehensive written test with questions on basic real estate transactions and laws affecting the sale of property. Licenses have to be renewed every year or two and may require continuing education classes or workshops.

Earnings

The average annual earnings of real estate agents is about $28,000, with the top 10 percent earning more than $78,600 per year. Few agents receive the entire commission on the sale of a home. Quite often they have to split the commission with other agents who represent the buyer or seller. Income usually increases as agents gain experience; however, their income fluctuates due to changing economic conditions.

A Successful Real Estate Agent

Marge Blake-Myers is a dynamic salesperson who recently sold more than $8 million worth of homes in a year. How did she do it? Marge says that she simply runs circles around most other real estate agents, working seven days a week and ten to twelve hours a day. This is what it takes to remain one of the top ten salespeople in a company of 125 agents for twenty-two years. It also takes a vibrant personality, someone who can work smoothly with hundreds of other salespeople and clients from all parts of the United States and even foreign countries. Plus, a very solid knowledge of the local real estate market is absolutely essential.

On a recent typical day, Marge got up at six o'clock and by eight had delivered her evaluations of new properties to a group of twenty real estate agents that meets weekly to share opinions of new listings. Then it was on to the home of a client to help choose a new carpet to make the home more appealing to prospective buyers. While the house was being measured, Marge was walking around taking notes for facts to put in the sales brochure. She also took a few minutes to arrange for a time when a house stager could stop by and make the house look its absolute best. Then on the way to the office, she stopped at the cleaners and a doughnut shop and listened to her voice mail messages on the car phone.

The hectic pace of Marge's day did not abate at the office. First, she met with another real estate agent to negotiate how much the seller would give her client for a new oven. Then she discussed offers that she had received on two of her listings with the agents making the offers for their clients. Marge faxed one offer to a client and sent the other to the colister of the property. Next, she left the office to deliver closing papers to a client as well as the money for the new oven from the successful completion of her earlier negotiations. Back in the office, Marge spent the rest of the day waiting for replies to the offers she had received earlier and making up a brochure for the home she had visited at the start of the day. She also directed her assistant to send computer printouts to clients who were looking for certain properties, arranged for a home inspection to be made, and spent the rest of her time catching up on the mountains of paperwork involved in the listing, buying, and selling of properties. While Marge spent a great part of this day in the office, the day before had been spent holding an open house in the afternoon, and the two preceding days were spent showing homes to clients.

Marge's Views on Being a Real Estate Agent. Marge loves her job because of the wonderful people she meets and because the job requirements meet her high-energy profile. As far as the future goes, she sees herself selling real estate far beyond the time when most people retire.

If you are contemplating a career as a real estate agent, you should realize that there are downsides. Marge points out that you face long hours, continual rejection, and tremendous pressure to produce. Also, it is difficult for young people to get started since there is no salary—only commissions. Furthermore, it is very difficult to have much free time for family and friends if you are going to be really successful.

Trading Stocks, Bonds, Commodities, and Options

A bell rings, and the action starts: traders yell, wave their hands, gesture with their fingers, and fight for a choice spot in a trading pit or post to get attention and make trades. This is what happens

Monday through Friday on the floors of exchanges handling the buying and selling of stocks, bonds, commodities, and options. These traders are using what is called the "open outcry" system, and adrenaline surges through their veins as long as the market is open. Also sharing in the frantic action are the brokers, who are using the traders to buy and sell financial products for their customers. While business is not conducted in the same way at all exchanges, the action is always fast-paced, from the opening to the closing of trading.

A Trader on the Pacific Stock Exchange

Mark Johnson is on the floor of the Pacific Stock Exchange from 6:30 A.M. to 1:10 P.M. Monday through Friday, buying and selling stock options. He works in a pit (a sunken area) with forty to fifty other traders and their clerks. He won't leave the pit until the end of a trading session even to eat lunch because he might miss a trade. Mark buys and sells stock options for approximately twelve stocks. A stock option is a contract conveying a right to buy or sell a stock at a specified price during a specific period of time.

Here's the way a trade works. A customer calls a broker to buy or sell a certain number of options. The broker places the order with the brokers on the floor of the options exchange, who send a broker to the pit where the options are being traded. The broker begins the trade by loudly asking: "How's the market in a specific stock option?" or "What's the market?" Then the traders who deal with that option yell out their prices. The broker then chooses the three traders in one, two, three order who are offering the best price. If Mark is chosen, he and the broker quickly decide on the size of the trade, and Mark gives the broker a ticket. Mark then turns around and hedges his position by buying or selling stock, which he does by yelling out an order to a stock clerk. The action moves at a lightning pace, and Mark could complete a transaction within five seconds. Trading continues until the bell rings at 1:10 P.M. to signal the end of the trading day.

Behind the Trading Scene. By 5:00 A.M., Mark is in the pit preparing for the opening of the exchange. The reason his work-day starts so early is that the Pacific Coast Exchange operates on the same hours as the New York Stock Exchange. The first thing Mark does is check the clearinghouse records of his trades from the day before to make sure they agree with his tickets. He then checks his current positions to figure out what needs to be adjusted that day.

When the market opens, Mark spends the rest of the day mak-ing two-sided markets (bid and offers) on the optionable stocks that he deals in. He makes markets based on supply and demand of the public, the current price of the stock, the direction the stock is moving (up or down), and his own position. Mark owns his own seat on the exchange; therefore, how successfully he trades determines entirely how much money he makes. The way he makes money is by taking advantage of the spread between the bid and offer price of options. In other words, to make money he buys options cheaper than he sells them for.

Getting Started. While you don't need to be a college graduate to become a trader, you do need to be a whiz at adding and sub-tracting fractions. Mark became fascinated with trading after taking a college class that involved the hypothetical trading of commodities. He also took a graduate course on option pricing. During this class, a guest lecturer who worked for the Pacific Stock Exchange spoke of career opportunities, and after graduation Mark started at the exchange as a quote operator and really began to learn how to trade.

In this job, Mark listened to what was happening in a pit and typed up the bids and offers so the public could see them on a screen and know where options were being priced. Then he learned even more about trading by clerking for a trader for two years. Mark's next step was to use the expertise he had acquired to start trading for himself.

Investment Banking

Having a career in investment banking means having a high-intensity, high-paying job. The primary business of investment banks is underwriting—the bringing together of investors with money and companies that need capital (money). They help large borrowers raise money quickly and efficiently. Investment banks purchase securities such as stocks and bonds from companies and then resell these securities in smaller quantities to investors. They are definitely not like the banks where you keep your savings or cash checks.

Investment banks often have brokerage operations—the buying and selling of stocks and bonds. Many of these banks also have mergers and acquisitions departments, which act as intermediaries in the buying and selling of companies or parts of companies. They package the company and suggest a sale price if they represent the seller and analyze a company and determine if it is being sold at a fair price if they represent the buyer. Some investment banks have real estate departments that bring together the buyers and sellers of large properties.

The Career Path

If you elect to work at an investment bank, you could work in any major city, such as Minneapolis, Chicago, or San Francisco. However, the largest investment banks are located in New York City, and most large investment banks also have offices there.

The starting position at an investment bank is usually as an analyst. You need to be a college graduate with an impressive resume to secure an analyst job, and you also need to exhibit an abundance of energy at your job interview. Investment banks hire interviewees who are sitting on the edge of their chairs and anxious to get started in banking.

These jobs pay well, with analysts having an average annual salary of $58,700, plus a substantial bonus after working a year. The analyst position is typically held for two or three years. Then most analysts go to business school to get their master's in business administration (M.B.A.).

The next rung up the ladder is associate. Most associates are hired after they have completed their M.B.A. degrees; however, a few become associates after working as analysts. Starting associates can expect to earn as much as $85,000 a year and can also earn excellent bonuses. After working as an associate for at least three years, the next career step is vice president. Some vice presidents go on to managing director positions; others often elect to take other jobs in the business world.

On the Job

Handling a job as an investment banker is a physical and mental challenge. You'll work from early in the morning to late at night—even all night at times, as well as on weekends. Project times are short, so you need to be truly focused, plus you are likely to handle more than one project at a time no matter what department of the bank you are working in. With each step up the career ladder, your hours on the job are reduced; however, the pace stays frantic. Even vice presidents work weekends from their homes and must have fax machines and computers and expect lots of conference calls.

Working at an Investment Bank in New York

Maude Clinton worked as an analyst at a prestigious investment bank for three years before leaving the firm to earn her M.B.A. This energetic analyst came to the bank with an impressive resume, including membership in Phi Beta Kappa and leadership roles in college extracurricular activities. Maude likes change and hates to be bored, so she wanted a high-energy job that would keep her busy at all times. She certainly found these things in her investment bank job, working twelve-hour days six or seven days a week as an analyst in equity capital markets, managing stock offerings for large corporations that wanted to sell stock to investors to get more capital for various reasons, such as building a new plant.

Maude worked as a liaison at the investment bank between the bank's sales force, which talked to investors, and the company wanting to sell stock. Her job was to get the two sides to agree on a price for the stock. It usually took two to three weeks to complete a deal, and she was always doing several deals at the same time.

Maude worked on the trading floor of her firm. She was on the job by 7:00 A.M. in a very noisy room with about two hundred other people, including analysts, salespeople, and traders. Everyone worked at a series of long desks and was allotted about three feet of space and a telephone. Between 7:30 A.M. and 4:00 P.M., analysts like Maude would call information over the loudspeaker, updating everyone on the stocks they were handling. She would tell the room when they were hoping to price a stock for a company, explain what kind of feedback she needed from the sales force, and tell the salespeople about opportunities to meet with the company wanting to sell stock.

Most of Maude's day was spent making phone calls. She spoke to stock salespeople all over the country, finding out what their investors thought of the company wanting to sell stock and asking how much of this stock the investors would buy. All of these indications of price and amount form what is known as "the book." Then with this information in hand, Maude would talk to the company and discuss a price. Finally, a deal would be made.

At investment banks, people typically work in teams. Maude worked with a partner of the firm in pricing the stocks and planning road shows—presentations in which the management of companies speak to prospective institutional investors about their companies with the purpose of encouraging investment. Maude worked with management at the company to plan what would be discussed at the road show.

A Glimpse at the Internet World

Today, it has been said that an Internet year is just one month in real time because technology is changing so fast. The Internet has become a career destination. In 2003, there were about 2.5 million Internet-related jobs. The people holding these jobs are young and energetic and willing to work long hours. They have the ability to do a variety of jobs and the drive and spirit necessary to start new businesses. All share a tremendous enthusiasm for this new medium of communication. New Internet businesses are opening every day, offering all kinds of products, from software to books to videos, and all kinds of services, from handling your banking chores to helping you find a job. All of these companies are looking for bright, energetic employees.

Two Brothers and Their Internet Business

Michael and David Mason are rapidly becoming seasoned owners of a business even though they are only in their twenties. With just $20,000 and the drive and determination to become entrepreneurs, they have established a successful Internet business selling books online within just two years. The focus of their business is getting books to customers as quickly as possible.

Establishing any business requires a great deal of energy. In order to get their business up and running, they had to learn sufficient programming skills to create most of what you see on their store's website. An experienced programmer was hired to do the more technical work involved in getting the inventory online and developing links for customers to explore. They also had to make arrangements with distributors to obtain books and secure access to the Net through a service provider.

The early months of their business were extremely busy, with the brothers working twelve-hour days and many weekends, as they were doing everything. Michael and David pulled orders from the website, placed them with the distributor (three-quarters of a mile away), picked up the orders from the distributor, and packaged and shipped the books the same day.

They were also answering e-mail, updating their online site, and doing all the paperwork associated with running a business. As their business became successful, more employees were hired.

Today, this energetic duo is busy searching for new markets for their books and growing their business. With success, they have cut back their work hours and no longer work on Sundays.

For More Information

The following organizations are helpful in learning more about careers in the business world:

Certified Masters of Business Administration
International Certification Institute
P.O. Box 8135
Greensboro, NC 27419
www.certifiedmba.com

Council for Entrepreneurial Development
P.O. Box 13353
Research Triangle Park, NC 27709
www.cednc.org

National Association for the Self-Employed
P.O. Box 612067
DFW Airport
Dallas, TX 75261
www.nase.org

National Association of Realtors
30700 Russell Ranch Road
Westlake Village, CA 91362
www.realtor.com

CHAPTER NINE

Assemble, Design, and Build

Careers in Manufacturing, Construction, and Maintenance

S ome 2.7 million people work in the manufacturing field assembling a variety of products. These employees often work on assembly lines that require them to move quickly while producing high-quality products. High-energy assemblers put together everything from cars, office machines, motors, television sets, and household appliances to airliners, spaceships, computers, and even missiles. Our clothing and shoes are manufactured, and much of our food is processed in plants.

Construction workers build and remodel homes, offices, shops, restaurants, and roads. They often work day and night and are able to complete a new home in just a few months. Auto manufacturers can assemble complex vehicles in only a few hours.

Once all these cars, homes, buildings, and roads have been manufactured or constructed, they need to be maintained. Cars have to be repaired, and homes and buildings need to be cleaned. To manufacture goods, build homes and offices, and keep them in tip-top shape, an army of workers is required. Many of these people have to work at full tilt all day long. These jobs are perfect for people with high energy levels.

....

Manufacturing

Henry Ford pioneered the use of assembly-line methods in putting together the famous Model T cars. Assembly lines may be more sophisticated today, with robots and automation; however, workers are still required to put together the parts of manufactured products. Typically, a product will move from station to station, with workers performing one or more tasks at each station, such as adding, tightening, welding, or inspecting a part. The process continues until a car, refrigerator, or barbecue grill has been manufactured. Assembly-line work varies from simple, repetitive jobs that are relatively easy to learn to those requiring great precision and many months of experience and training.

Today's assembly lines often are composed of teams of people who work together at stations to complete one or more tasks before a product goes to the next station. Assemblers have also had to learn to work with robots, computers, and sophisticated equipment. Nevertheless, whether an assembler is putting together an airline meal, a car, or a toaster, the pace is always fast, and there is always one product after another moving down an assembly line or arriving at a workstation. These jobs need high-energy people who can do accurate work quickly with pauses only for breaks and meals.

What It's Like to Work on an Assembly Line

Gayle Bowen began her career at NUMMI, assembling Toyota Corollas and Geo Prizms. It isn't easy to get a job on the assembly line at NUMMI. After turning in her application, Gayle had to take mechanical and math tests, be interviewed informally, and take blood and urine tests—all on the same day. Then a week later, she was called back to take more tests. This time she had to put nuts and bolts together as fast as she could on a simulation test. She also had to put tape on the side of a car to show she could line the tape up so the car could be painted. There was also a test to see whether she could follow instructions exactly.

The next week she went back and sat down with five people at a table, and they solved different problems together to show they could work as a team. After another personal interview and a physical examination, she got a job on the assembly line.

For her first assembly-line job, Gayle was assigned to a five-person team that had five different jobs to do as they set windshields into cars. Her first job was to put on the left side molding. The other jobs were setting the right and left sides of the windshield, putting on the right side molding, and building up the glass. Gayle had fifty-eight seconds to do her job. The team also had to go to another area and do repair work on windshields that did not pass the windshield leak test.

For the first two and a half years on this job, Gayle worked the swing shift, from 4:30 P.M. to 1:00 A.M. Later on, she worked the day shift, between 6:00 A.M. and 2:30 P.M. The assembly line only stopped when it was time for a break or a meal or when there were problems with machinery. Gayle worked intervals of two and a half hours before the line stopped for fifteen minutes for a break or forty-five minutes for a meal.

Climbing the Career Ladder. After one and a half years as a windshield assembler, Gayle went to the final line and worked on car interiors. This job was a little easier, as she didn't get in and out of cars as much and did not have as much heavy lifting to do. Gayle also become a team leader after going through a selection process and attending class for forty hours on her own time to learn leadership techniques.

Gayle's next step up the career ladder was to become a quality assurance team member. In this job, she worked by herself checking more than one hundred items on finished cars. When she found a defect, she was usually able to repair it herself. Gayle continued to climb the career ladder and became a Toyota production systems trainer, working with both new hires and team leaders.

Today, she has a challenging job on the pilot team. After the designers create a new model, it is the task of pilot team members to make sure that the product can be built smoothly on the different assembly lines. Gayle goes to Japan to see the way they do it, and then comes back and revamps the process to work in her plant. She is responsible for seeing that the process flows. This means checking that the parts fit well, the jobs are ergonomically right, and the timing is correct.

Special Training. Before Gayle ever went out on the floor, there was a week of orientation, during which she learned about company policies and labor relations. As part of the training, different group leaders gave classes on standardized work and teamwork. When she finally went out on the floor, Gayle spent the first hour watching how a left side molding was put on cars. She was given a manifest (a large sheet of paper with instructions for building the vehicle) to read so she would know a Corolla from a Prizm and which part each car got. Then gradually throughout the day, doing a little at a time, she learned how to do her job under the supervision of the team leader. For three days, the team leader stayed with her, giving help as needed. Within sixty days, Gayle had learned all five of the team jobs. And within ninety days, she knew how to do repair work when it was needed.

The Team Approach. The NUMMI plant where Gayle works uses the team approach, as so many other manufacturing companies do. Team members at NUMMI know how to do all of the team jobs and actually rotate the jobs. As a team member, Gayle had the responsibility for getting her job done and seeing that the group got its job done. If someone missed part of a job, she told that person, and she also helped out if anyone fell behind. Under the team approach, team members share responsibility with all the teams working together to build a car. If Gayle saw an earlier problem while doing her job, she would pull what is called the "andon" cord. A light would go off in the area she had indicated, and the team leader for that area would come over to find out what the problem was. For Gayle, working on a team meant far more than working together. Her team would celebrate team members' birthdays and help each other when someone felt out of sorts. She found that team spirit was infectious, too. If someone started singing, everyone on the whole line joined in. This happened a lot during the holidays.

A Closer Look at Job Opportunities and Earnings

The employment of assembly-line workers is expected to grow slowly through 2010 as automation increases and more manufacturing is done overseas, where labor costs are lower. Assembly-line jobs that can be performed more cheaply by automated equipment will disappear. Nevertheless, those who do precision assembly work in hard-to-reach places like airplane cockpits will not easily be replaced by technology.

Many assembly-line workers are members of labor unions whose wages are set by contracts between the unions and manufacturers. However, the union movement has declined in recent years, and even cars are now being manufactured in nonunion plants. Wages vary enormously for assembly-line workers, with some in unskilled jobs only earning minimum wage and a few earning close to $1,000 a week.

Construction

Whenever you see a road, home, or building being constructed, you can be sure that there is pressure to get the job completed on schedule. Construction contracts usually have deadlines telling when the work must be completed and may also have penalties if the work is not finished on time. Construction companies seek high-energy people who are willing to work long hours and do physically demanding labor in all kinds of weather and conditions. Construction workers may be working in the freezing cold of Minnesota in the winter and the heat of Texas in the summer. They can be perched on top of a girder on a skyscraper, crawling in tunnels, or working with dangerous equipment. On the job, they may need to wear safety clothing such as gloves and hard hats and devices to protect their eyes, mouth, and ears. Job shifts can be twelve hours long, and it may even be necessary to work at night if work has fallen behind schedule or the workplace cannot be accessed in the daytime, as with construction on busy roads.

Civil Engineers

This is the oldest branch of engineering and deals with the design and supervision of the construction of roads, airports, tunnels, bridges, water supply and sewage systems, and buildings. About one-third of all civil engineers work for federal, state, or local government agencies. Civil engineers work at construction sites, and many move from place to place on different projects. The job outlook is favorable for civil engineers through 2010 because of the expanding economy and the need to design, construct, repair, and replace so many public structures, from roads to water supply and pollution control systems.

Starting salaries for civil engineers with bachelor's degrees are more than $40,000 a year. The median salary for all civil engineers is about $55,700 a year. Engineers with master's degrees have starting annual salaries of about $44,000, and those with doctorates may start at about $62,000 per year.

Moving Equipment Operators

Generally, moving equipment operators use machinery to move materials and dirt short distances around a construction site. The equipment they operate is very expensive ($1 million for a crane, $100,000 or more for a bulldozer). It is very easy to damage the equipment if you don't know what you are doing.

Most operators learn on the job under the guidance of experienced operators. Some are trained in formal union apprentice programs. In either case, you need a good sense of balance, the ability to judge distance, and good hand-eye coordination. It helps also if you have mechanical aptitude because you may perform some maintenance work on the equipment you are operating.

The number of job openings for moving equipment operators fluctuates widely from year to year because the construction industry is so sensitive to economic conditions. Wages do vary from area to area and are usually higher in metropolitan areas. Median weekly earnings of crane, grader, dozer, and scraper operators are nearly $700. Annual earnings can be limited, however, when bad weather causes construction projects to shut down.

Building a New Highway

A recent example of a project done by a large national construction company is the building of an interstate highway in Florida. At the job site, the weather was frequently hot and humid, and rain often caused delays in completion. This project was scheduled to take two and a half years to complete at a cost of $52 million. Approximately ninety people, including engineers, heavy equipment operators, carpenters, and laborers were involved in building this section of highway, and about one hundred pieces of equipment were used.

Bill McGowan was one of two field engineers on this project. All of the field and office engineers report to the project engineer, who is responsible for every aspect of the project. As his title indicates, Bill is out in the field. He handles the grading of the highway, while the other field engineer is responsible for the structures and bridges. It is Bill's job to make sure that the highway is built right. Doing this job is decidedly one that requires a great deal of energy. Besides needing to be in twenty places at once, Bill is on the job by 6:00 A.M. and doesn't leave until 6:00 P.M. or later. When the crew works at night on the highway, he is on the job from 7:00 P.M. to 6:00 A.M.

A Day on the Job. Typically, Bill spends time planning his workday when he first arrives at the office. Then at 6:30 A.M., he attends a meeting with all the management staff to discuss coordination issues and how to use the people and equipment that day. After the meeting, he goes out into the field to help the crews get the day's operation going and to supervise the layout of where the road will go. Bill spends the day driving a four-wheel-drive pickup around the highway job, which has activity all along the nine miles of road being built. He is constantly looking for ways to improve the productivity and efficiency of the operation. Much time is spent talking to foremen and superintendents about what is to be built and how it will be built. This necessitates reading and interpreting plans for them. Often, he is so busy that there is no time for lunch. While the work crew usually leaves at 4:30 P.M., Bill stays on, wrapping up the work he has done during the day, writing reports, or planning for the night shift if there will be one.

Bill's Career Path. Bill has a master's degree in civil engineering and construction management. He started his career in an entry-level position as an assistant to an office engineer. During this office job, Bill learned the business side of construction. This involved learning how different jobs were maintained, and it prepared him to handle all kinds of variables and unknowns when he was out on the job. He spent this time keeping track of costs on different jobs and providing production reports to management. Bill's next job was as a field engineer on a road-building job in Texas. Then he worked in the same capacity building a toll road in Southern California before he was assigned to the Florida highway project.

Bulldozer Operator

On a highway job, bulldozer operators arrive at the work site ten minutes before their shift begins. Before a dozer is started, the operator checks all the oil and fluid levels on the machine. Once a dozer is fired up, the operator begins pushing dirt to construct the new highway and keeps pushing dirt all day under the direction of a foreman. The dirt must be moved as quickly as possible. The more experienced the operators are, the better they are at this job. They work from 7:00 A.M. to 11:30 A.M., with a fifteen-minute break. Then after a half-hour lunch, they work until 4:30 P.M., with another fifteen-minute break.

This is a very dangerous job in an environment that is hot, dusty, and loud. Bulldozer operators must always be on their toes and looking around to avoid hurting themselves or others. Throughout the workday, they are moving their hands and feet in coordination on the levers and pedals to maneuver the dozer. Their days go quickly, however, because they are so busy.

Building Homes, Offices, and Other Structures

One of the key figures in construction is the carpenter, who cuts, fits, and assembles wood and other materials to build many different structures. You'll find carpenters building forms for the construction of highways, dams, and bridges. You'll find them building, renovating, and modernizing homes and offices. Typically, carpenters work from blueprints or instructions from supervisors. They measure, mark, and arrange materials. Then they cut and shape the materials using tools such as chisels, planes, saws, drills, and sanders. Next, they join the materials together with nails, screws, staples, and adhesives. In the final step, they check the accuracy of their work with levels, rules, plumbs, and framing squares. Their job is much easier if they are working with prefabricated components. Being a carpenter is strenuous work, like other jobs in the building trades. Carpenters are always standing, climbing, bending, and kneeling.

Most carpenters learn the trade through on-the-job training; it is also possible to enter the field through training programs or apprenticeships. As a carpenter, you may change employers every time you finish a construction job. Or, like many carpenters, you can alternate between working for a contractor and working as a contractor on small jobs. Top carpenters can earn more than $1,100 a week. Jobs will be plentiful for carpenters through 2010.

A Successful Building Contractor

Greg Abbott lives and works in a suburban community in the San Francisco Bay Area, where he owns a company that specializes in building additions on homes, as well as renovating and modernizing homes. Besides being a skilled carpenter, Greg holds a general contractor's license, which lets him do electrical and plumbing work. Most of the time Greg works alone, but he does hire a helper at times, and he also hires subcontractors to do special work such as laying floors, roofing, and pouring concrete.

Greg's life as a contractor is a busy one. While he is working on a job, he is also soliciting new jobs, as well as getting building permits. Greg always carries a cell phone with him so he is never out of touch with potential clients and can just pick up the phone and order any materials he may need. Because he is self-employed, the more work Greg does, the more he will earn. This is definitely not a job for a couch potato.

Greg may work for a month or more putting an addition on a home, or he may be able to complete a job installing new windows in just a day or two. His work is almost always varied. Typically, it includes some carpentry, but Greg may also find himself laying tile, hanging a light fixture, installing a new kitchen sink, or even painting. On many days, his work is interrupted with trips to get lumber or other materials for a job. There are also breaks to talk to building inspectors, and sometimes he has to stop by a previous job to complete some work that he wasn't able to finish earlier. From the time Greg's day begins around eight o'clock until it ends at approximately five o'clock, he rarely stops working except for lunch. Then, in the evenings, he has to spend time making estimates, costing jobs, writing proposals, and returning phone calls. His wife handles all the bookkeeping and the writing of contracts.

A Remodeling Job. You will be able to appreciate the variety Greg encounters in his work by looking at this list of tasks that he had to do in remodeling a dining room, kitchen, family room, and study. This work was completed in a month.

1. Remove existing dining room wall
2. Extend floor and frame new walls for dining room
3. Install exterior siding and two windows
4. Sheetrock, tape, and texture new wall
5. Remove existing lower kitchen cabinet
6. Reinstall lower cabinet, and install new upper cabinet
7. Tile countertop to match existing kitchen
8. Remove bar cabinet in family room
9. Tape family room wall for paint
10. Move plumbing and install bar cabinets in study
11. Install new doors at kitchen and at nook
12. Install new hardwood floor to match existing

Roofing Contractors

Roofs can leak and need to be repaired or replaced. Also, new homes and buildings have to be roofed. This strenuous, high-energy work is done outdoors in all kinds of weather, and roofs are extremely hot places to be in the summer. The job involves heavy lifting as well as climbing, bending, and kneeling, and it is always fast paced. It is essential to be in good shape to handle this job.

Roofers can expect plentiful job opportunities through 2010. About three-fourths of all roofers work for roofing contractors. The rest are self-employed. Wages vary by region. Pay is highest in metropolitan areas. On average, roofers earn about $15.50 per hour. Top earners receive an hourly rate of about $26.00.

Keeping Places Clean and in Good Condition

Go to the yellow pages of almost any telephone directory and notice how many cleaning services there are. You will find many small companies and a few franchises offering residential, commercial, home, and apartment cleaning, plus such special services as carpet and window cleaning, spring cleaning, move in/out cleaning, and daily, weekly, and monthly cleaning. All of these firms offer jobs for cleaners or janitors. Many of these firms are small, and besides running the business and supervising workers, the owners also step in and do some of the cleaning work. Cleaners and janitors can also find jobs with schools, hospitals, stores, and other businesses.

Being a cleaner or janitor is a high-energy job because you need to work fast and are on your feet most of the time. It's strenuous too, as you are often bending, stooping, and stretching to dust, mop, sweep, and lift or push furniture or equipment. No special training is needed for this job, with most people learning the necessary skills on the job. Climbing the career ladder in this job is limited to large firms that employ many cleaners and janitors. Then it is possible to become a supervisor. There is also the possibility of owning your own firm. If you work full-time as a cleaner or janitor, you can expect to earn about $400 a week.

For More Information

For more information about careers in manufacturing, construction, and maintenance, contact societies, unions, and professional associations. The following organizations should provide helpful information:

CIVIL ENGINEERING
American Society of Civil Engineers
1801 Alexander Bell Drive
Reston, VA 20191
www.asce.org

MOVING EQUIPMENT OPERATORS
International Union of Operating Engineers
1125 Seventeenth Street NW
Washington, DC 20036
www.iuoe.org

CARPENTERS

Associated General Contractors of America
333 John Carlyle Street, Suite 200
Alexandria, VA 22314
www.agc.org

CLEANERS AND JANITORS

Building Service Contractors Association International
10201 Lee Highway, Suite 225
Fairfax, VA 22030
www.bscai.org

CHAPTER TEN

Even More Jobs for High-Energy Types

Peppy people with high energy are willing to go the extra mile; they don't mind being on their feet for a whole shift, working a sixty-hour week, or doing several tasks at once. The purpose of this book is to give you ideas about careers that will let you use your abundance of energy on the job. Of course, there are many more careers than those that have been mentioned in this book. You may have to be creative to find some of them. Try browsing through an occupational handbook and consider the energy requirements of the many jobs that are listed. Do the same thing while reading want ads in newspapers or surfing through online job listings. You'll discover even more jobs that require people to stay on their toes all day long while they work as clowns, aerobics instructors, professional ice-skaters, auctioneers, flight attendants, tour leaders, cruise company employees, and computer programmers. Here are a few more careers that could be quite satisfying to high-energy types who want to be on the go throughout the workday.

Flight Attendants

You simply can't sit down on the job when you are a flight attendant, except for takeoffs and landings. The entire seventy-five to eighty-five hours a month that you are in the air are spent catering to your passengers' needs. Let's go aboard a United Airlines flight from San Francisco to Hong Kong with Linda Curtis

Olinger to see what actually happens on the job during this fifteen-hour flight. About one and three-quarters hours before the flight is scheduled to leave, Linda arrives at the airport to prepare for the flight. She learns her assignment at the flight briefing, then takes the very long walk to the international terminal and boards the plane.

Once aboard the plane, Linda quickly stows her gear, checks out the emergency equipment in her area, and starts getting the first-class cabin, where she typically works, ready for the passengers. She checks the cleanliness of the cabin and makes sure there are enough headsets, amenities kits, pillows, blankets, and current newspapers. When the passengers start coming aboard, she welcomes them, hangs up their coats, helps them stow their luggage, and provides them with beverages. This occupies all of her time until takeoff.

After takeoff, when it is safe to do so, Linda gets up and checks to see whether the passengers in her section are warm enough because the cabin can become cool. It's also time to serve beverages, take entree orders, and hand out headphones to those who wish to watch the onboard movies. The dinner service typically takes about three hours. Once it is completed, Linda and the other attendants tidy up, then they take turns having breaks, which means a stint for Linda of being the only attendant in the section. During this time, she is busy serving beverages (especially water), making coffee, and possibly selling duty-free merchandise. In the middle of the night, Linda and the other attendants prepare and serve a snack, and they serve another meal one and a half hours before landing.

After the plane has landed in Hong Kong, Linda helps the passengers gather the belongings that they have stowed and helps them off the plane. Then she leaves the plane and takes a bus to the hotel. Linda stays in Hong Kong for forty hours before she boards a flight back to San Francisco.

Teachers and School Administrators

Something is always happening in the classroom when you are a teacher—discussions, lectures, group work, projects, demonstrations, computer activities, games, speeches, reports, movies, slide shows, and quizzes. Then when the school day is over, there are tests to prepare, papers to grade, lessons to plan, meetings with parents and the school staff, help sessions for students, reports to complete, and extracurricular activities to lead. Whether teachers work with five- or sixteen-year-olds, their days are full of activities. It is not just teachers who have busy days; so do principals, who work with teachers, students, parents, and people in the community.

A High School Music Teacher

Thomas Dick always has long, busy days that usually extend into the evening in his job as orchestra director at a large suburban high school. During the school day, he teaches four periods of strings and one period of wind and percussion instruments each day. Then four evenings a week, Thomas supervises rehearsals of different sections of the orchestra after school. And every Tuesday evening he holds a three-hour rehearsal of performance and possible contest pieces to discover problems that the students can work on at home and in their sections.

During the school year, he is often a guest conductor for junior and senior high school orchestras and acts as a judge at several music contests. He also finds time to serve on the board of the state school music association. In the summer, Thomas often acts as the orchestra director of a summer music camp. During his teaching career, he has also at various times played the cello with different symphony groups and directed choirs. It definitely takes energy to handle Thomas's teaching job, but it is made much easier because he loves music and teaching music to his students.

A High School Principal

William Duke describes his work environment as principal of a large suburban high school as busy, rather exciting, fun, demanding, and varied. It is a twelve-month-a-year job with such a volume of work that it is impossible for him to catch up easily on all his work, especially the paperwork, if he takes too much time off.

Every day is different for a principal. William quite often finds himself doing things that were not on his daily to-do list. He arrives at school around 7:00 A.M. and spends the time before school starts walking around talking with the teachers and students. He likes to be visible to everyone.

Then he usually has administrative meetings with different directors and deans. He spends his lunch hour in the cafeteria, keeping his finger on the pulse of what is happening in the school. From 3:30 to 5:30 P.M. is the most productive time of day for him, as he is able to work without interruption on tasks that need to get done.

Three or four nights a week, he returns to the school to attend games, performing arts events, awards banquets, school board meetings, and committee meetings. On weekends, he attends the different sporting events that the school teams are participating in, from soccer to basketball, and he pitches in wherever he is needed. You may even see him help park cars in the school parking lot.

Farmers

Lawrence Olson was raised on a farm and was doing daily chores after school when he was eight years old. By the time he was twelve, he was operating all the farm equipment. After he finished a tour of duty in the U.S. Air Force, Lawrence rented eighty acres and began farming. Over the next thirty years, this grower of soybeans and corn acquired an additional 860 acres of land.

Lawrence does almost all the work on his farm. His work is seasonal because of the types of crops he grows. From March to May, he is busy preparing the soil and planting his crops. He works in the fields from dawn until it is too dark to see. The summer months aren't quite as busy a time, as Lawrence works forty to fifty hours a week preparing for harvesting his crops. September is extremely busy because this is harvest season. The rest of the year, his workload is quite light, and he spends his time repairing equipment and planning for the next season's crops. If he were to raise livestock, his workload would be heavy every day, as animals must be fed and watered daily year-round.

Aerobics Teachers

Tammy Smith teaches aerobics. From the moment the music starts to signal the beginning of one of her classes until it is over, she is constantly in motion. While she is leading a class, she is always smiling and encouraging her students to keep up with her. Besides teaching classes, this very peppy person trains with other teachers at the YMCA where she works and takes frequent classes to learn new routines.

Tammy is well prepared for this career. In college she majored in physical fitness and taught an aerobics class for two years. Then she took special classes to learn how to put moves together and to stretch properly. It was also necessary for her to obtain certificates in CPR and aerobics instruction in order to be hired by the YMCA. In the future, she would like to open her own studio.

Water Directors

Deli Caho came to the YMCA as a class participant and ended up becoming the director of the water program. In any given week, Deli spends much of her time in the pool teaching three water aerobics classes, three arthritis exercise classes, six classes for day care groups, and two classes for home-school programs. As director, she spends one hour a day answering phone calls about the water program. Deli also sets the work schedule for swim instructors and lifeguards, lesson plans, and skill sheets. In addition, she maintains a card file for swim lessons, holds monthly workshops for aqua aerobics teachers, and schedules parties for groups that want to rent the pool. Deli directs a staff of twelve part-time employees.

Fishers

Dennis Forbes is the captain of a ninety-foot fishing boat that he uses to catch sole, channel rockfish, sablefish, ling and rock cod, and halibut in the Pacific Ocean. He learned the trade by going out on weekends with commercial fishers because they wanted company.

Today, Dennis is on the ocean from 120 to 140 days a year. Each trip, he stays out from three to six days, depending on how many fish he and his crew of three helpers catch. As skipper, he makes all the decisions, including where they will go, what gear will be put down, what nets will be used, and how much wire will be put down.

Once the fishing area is reached, Dennis and the crew never stop working except to sleep from four to six hours a day. Besides catching the fish, they must immediately ice the fish properly. Dennis's work does not stop when he comes back to shore. The fish must be unloaded, and the boat needs to be cleaned. Repairs are made to the fishing gear, and the fuel filters on the engine are changed. Then it is time to buy groceries and ice for another trip. Fishing is a twelve-month job that requires individuals who love this lifestyle. There also are a lot of dangers—Dennis has had three of his boats sink.

Trek Leaders

Peggy Day leads treks to exotic locales and has walked from one end of the Himalayas to the other. She specializes, however, in leading treks to Bhutan, a small country that lies between India and Tibet. Peggy arranges every aspect of a trek. She devises the itinerary, arranges the air travel and land accommodations, secures visas, and contacts the Bhutanese who will help her with the trek. Peggy's treks last from one to three weeks. Her groups walk and hike under her direction while looking for wildlife and admiring the magnificent scenery.

You definitely have to be in good shape to lead a Himalayan trek, as well as to participate in one, because you are walking on rugged trails from seven thousand to thirteen thousand feet in elevation. You will not have to carry supplies for camping out, as they are carried by pack animals. Cooks and helpers accompany the trekkers, as well as a representative of a Bhutan tour company. Peggy is in charge of all these people, as well as the trekkers. She is constantly thinking ahead to keep the trek running smoothly.

Peggy spends about half of the year trekking. She has had to learn the local customs and traditions of Bhutan plus some of the native language, even though English is the primary language in the schools. What she likes most about this job is that trekking has given her friends throughout the world who have shared the memorable experience of trekking with her.

Executive Hairdressers

After graduating from college in Indiana, Kenn Williams attended cosmetology training school and started on a career that has been jammed with activity ever since. First, he went to New York City, where he became an apprentice of the famous stylist Vidal Sassoon. Then it was on to London with Sassoon to further his career and learn more about color and cutting work. Next, Kenn returned to New York City to work for CBS and off-Broadway productions, concentrating on makeup. After a while, he decided to return to Indiana to be near his family and work in a salon that featured him as a celebrity stylist. His next move was to a salon that is part of a chain, where he continued improving his cutting, coloring, and makeup skills. After a stint of five years with this salon, Kenn went to the West Coast to NBC and then worked on makeup for the Planet of the Apes movies. After working on all of these movies, he returned to Indiana, where he has remained ever since as a salon owner.

Not content with just owning a salon, Kenn also went into clothing design and did fashion commentary on a local TV station. He also began traveling for the next eight to ten years to educational shows around the country, where he and a partner gave instruction on hair, makeup, and clothing. Today, Kenn has become what is known in his profession as an executive hairdresser, meaning that he owns and manages a shop, works behind a chair, and trains new hairdressers. In order to accomplish everything that he does, it is necessary for him to work close to eighty-hour weeks. Kenn's days begin between 8:30 and 9:15 A.M., and he may still be at his salon as late as 10:00 P.M. some evenings. Much of that time is spent cutting, coloring, and styling the hair of his devoted clientele, which extends to the third generation in some families. Kenn is also busy devising ways to offer more personalized services in his salon, including skin care and massage. At least one day a month, Kenn teaches his craft at a school. For almost forty years, he has been a hairdresser, and this extremely energetic individual believes that he will end his career as a teacher, sharing his experiences with the next generation of hairdressers.

Animal Control Officers

When you are an animal control officer like Linda Adams, you had better be prepared to run on the job because that is what you need to do to catch stray dogs. To get this job, she was required to have knowledge of animals; a law enforcement background that included course work in arrest, search, seizure, and citation authority; firearms training; and the ability to drive a truck. Linda had gained these skills through college classes and her previous work as a ranger.

On the job, Linda wears a law enforcement uniform, a badge, and a nametag. She carries pepper spray and a baton. When Linda climbs behind the wheel of her truck for a day in the field, she knows her day will be full of activity because she has the following responsibilities:

- Patrol city parks; watch for dogs off leash
- Handle animal emergencies such as removing animals from hot cars
- Pick up dogs running loose
- Answer complaints about problem animals (such as a barking dog)
- Pick up stray animals
- Enforce licensing regulations
- Handle dog bites
- Investigate animal welfare and cruelty
- Pick up food donations for the animal shelter
- Pick up animals in response to euthanasia requests
- Trap wildlife

Throughout the day, Linda is in and out of her truck and running a lot as she chases dogs. Also, when she takes an animal back to the shelter, she must give it a health check, weigh and worm the animal, and make a record of it.

On days when she is in the office, she is busy working with animal adoption, cleaning the shelter, giving educational talks, and handling the licensing of animals. This career requires a strong and vigorous person who is also capable of handling the emotional situations encountered in this work.

Child Care Workers

Lois Spencer is an assistant teacher at a child care center operated by a national chain. The general guidelines for her busy day caring for eight one-year-olds in her section are spelled out by the chain and include very few moments when she is not expected to be doing something. At the start of her day at 8:00 A.M., she is usually sitting on the floor with one or two of the young children, playing, talking, or reading to them. At about 9:00 A.M. she prepares a snack and serves it to the children. Then Lois goes outside and closely supervises the children as they play on the playground. Lunch is served to these very young children at 10:30 A.M. Although Lois does not prepare the meal, she is extremely busy providing the children with feeding assistance. After lunch, the children have another short stint outdoors before they are diapered and put down for their naps. During nap time, Lois straightens the room, washes each child's cup or bottle, sets up sleeping cots for the older children at the center, and does projects for the director. Then she has time for her lunch.

When the children start to wake up, Lois reads to them or introduces quiet games until all are awake. Next, they may do movements to music or play with clay. Then, it is time for everyone to be diapered again before a snack is served. After snack time, Lois supervises another outdoor playtime. When they return to the classroom, she does individual activities with the children as parents begin to arrive. Her busy day is supposed to end at 5:00 P.M., but she doesn't leave until all the children in her section are gone for the day.

About the Authors

Marjorie Eberts and Margaret Gisler have been writing together professionally for twenty-four years. They are prolific freelance authors with more than seventy books in print. Besides writing more than twenty career books, the two authors have written textbooks, beginning readers, and study skills books for schoolchildren. They also write a syndicated education column, "Dear Teacher," which appears in newspapers throughout the country. Maria Olson has written four career books and is currently employed as a logistics expert for a major manufacturing company.

Writing this book was a special pleasure for the authors as it gave them the opportunity to talk to so many high-energy people who have exciting, fast-paced careers. The authors firmly believe that they are high-energy types. Eberts and Gisler have already written three new books this year; they write their nationally syndicated column each week; and they handle their teaching assignments. Gisler has also established a literacy foundation, and Olson works action-filled days in the business world.

Marjorie Eberts is a graduate of Stanford University, and Margaret Gisler is a graduate of Ball State and Butler Universities. Both received their specialist degrees in education from Butler University. Margaret is currently studying for her doctorate in education at Ball State University. Maria Olson is a graduate of Indiana University with a bachelor's degree in business.